A Note to My Black Son...

by Toya L. Adams-Driscal, MEd.

BLACK KIDS MATTER

Illustrations by Rodney Potts
Foreword by Dawn M. Gay
Cover illustrations by Jessica Stevenson

Black Mom & Son Illustration By: Rodney Potts

To All the Black Moms who contributed to this project: THANK YOU from the depths of my heart and soul. This could have never been possible without you and your loving words of wisdom to not only your Black Son but to EVERY Black Son who might read these encouraging, inspiriting, loving words. May God continue to richly bless you and your Black Sons!

Sincerely,

Toya Adams-Driscal, Med.

This book is dedicated to all the Black Sons of the world, especially mine:

Mason Xavier Charles Driscal

In loving memory of Charles Edward Adams, a Black Son affectionately known to me as Uncle Billy

When I was asked to write the foreword for **A Note to My Black Son...** I was both honored and challenged because this is such a necessary piece of literature. As the Mother of Daughters, I have always spoke to my Daughters about how great they are as Black Girls and the contribution they bring to the world. My Daughters have always been a part of a world where they are usually the minority and I find it important that they are proud and confident in who they are. I was led to write a book for little Black Girls (**Black Girls Are Magical**) that speaks affirmation to them, to our culture, and to our overall presence as Black Girls. When I read the book to my daughters for the first time, immediately following one of them said to me "Mommy, what about Black Boys?" At that very moment I realized how much our Young Black Men are in need to hear the same affirmations and reminders of how great they are. I realized that we put more emphasis on uplifting our Black Girls and Women than we do in supporting and uplifting our Black Boys and Men.

We live in a society that depicts our Black Boys as having no positive contribution to the world we live in. The world around us does not encourage them to be great, to be educated, remind them of their worth, or validate them. It is our duty as parents and as a culture to protect our Black Boys, guide them, and to speak as much life into them as we do our Black Girls. I had no idea how I could be a benefit to the needs of our young Kings, but God placed the vision on the heart of my sister. When Toya reached out to me to discuss her vision, I was beyond excited! I was excited for her, I was excited for the Black Boys this project would touch, and I was excited knowing the magnitude of how things move when we collectively touch and agree. **A Note to My Black Son...** speaks life, praise, and honor to the inner souls of Young Black Men who will one day lead our world. It is a necessary literature in the homes of Black Boys and Men to remind them of their greatness and that they matter in our lives and in our world. They need to know that they are needed for our survival as Black People.

Acknowledgment of Contributing Black Moms

Afrika Gupton-Jones

Andratesha Fritzgerald

Angel Jackson-Berry

Angela Landers

Angela Vann

Arianne Hennighan

Ashley N. Hawthorne, Med.

Asia Jordan

Bonita D. Henderson

Bre'shae

Brianna Riley

Dr. Brittany Clark-Lyons

Carnesha Bates

Chavone Taylor-Nash

Cheryl L. Wright

Cicely D. Campbell

Courtney Bean-Jones

Dalanda Jackson, MEd.

Danielle M. Birch

Danielle Green-Welch, MEd., EdS.

Danielle T. Simmons-Harrell

Dayrnice M. Chavis

Denise West

Dominica Drake

Ericka M. Hicks

Erma V. Robinson

Eunice Sipp

Evette Jackson-Clark

Felicia Douglas

Felicia Limage

Goddezz Sadaqa Calhoun-Redus

Hollie Bodiford-Taylor

Hope Sheppard

Janay Bailey

Jasmine Robinson

Jayla D.

Kyra J. Hall, MEd.

Leatrice Clark

Ms. Londa M. Byrd

Malika Brown

Marilyn K. Haynes

Marlene L. Barbee

Marlene C. Cole

Mary I. Tella

Maxine E. P. White

Melonn R. Blue. Momager & Entrepreneur

Mendi Joi Carrington

Michelle Gayles

Miriam Basnight-Sterling

Natasha Cox

Nicole Goode, Jalon's Mom

Nicole H.

Pamela Smith

Robyn Nicole Durr-Henry

Robyn Hildreth

Sashelle Thomas Alexander, PhD.

Shauna Scott-Rose

Shaundallah Rogers

Sherrell Britt-Turner

Sheryl (Smith) Thomas-Washburn

Tara Driscal

Tiffany D. Golden

Tracy H.

Zykina Lafaye Stewart

A Note to My Black Son Mason, My Sweet Pea…

From the moment I found out I was pregnant; I have loved you! You are the best part of me, and I thank God for allowing me to be chosen as your Mom. You have always had a special "light" that allows you to continually shine brightly in a universe of darkness. I pray that you will always find a way to tap into your "light" and shine on everyone and everything around you. Your smile and your laugh are my absolute favorites; you bring true joy into my life. Even in my darkest moments, you have always been a beacon lighting my way back; you are the reason I believe that no matter what might come my (our) way, it will be alright!

You have shown me what true love and sacrifice are and I am thankful for that. You teach me every day how to be a better person because of the positive examples that I have been charged to set for you. I know that you are watching my every move and I must be extremely careful of my words and actions. I pray that God will continue to give me the strength to help mold you into the man that will continue to make me the proud Mom that I already am.

People always comment about how talented you are, and I am humbled by their wonderful words about your gifts you share so willingly with the world: dancing, singing and acting. I have always said, "One day, Mason's name will appear in rolling credits or a marquee somewhere!" and I sincerely believe it with my whole heart. You danced in the womb and have not stopped since; I love your fearlessness and confidence to dance at ANYTIME and ANYPLACE. I want you to continue to embrace your talents and hone them no matter what others might say good or bad. Always follow your dreams wherever they may lead you!

As your Mom, it is my job to lift you up when you are down, protect you from danger, speak life into you when feeling deflated and love you without conditions; I pray that you always feel those things from me. I promise to always do my absolute best to encourage you and set a positive example for you to follow. In a world that will always try to steal your innocence, make you feel inferior and cause you not only mental, emotional and possibly physical harm, I will always be the warm, loving place you need to lay your head and your troubles down to rest.

*I pray that you follow the calling that has been placed on your life by God; you are fearfully and wonderfully made and you know the truth about you no matter what anyone else might have to say about you. Your compassion and genuine concern for those you love is unmatched; hold on to that and always remember: **Jeremiah 29:11** (NIV) "For I know that plans I have for you," declares the Lord, "plans to prosper you and not to harm you, plans to give you hope and a future."*

Love Always…Mommy

Photo By: Kelli A. Newsom of KelliVision Photography

A Note to My Black Son Sidney Austin...

I never planned on being a mother. We did not even plan on having a child, but God knew exactly what I needed when we were blessed with you. Since the day you were born you have been teaching me. Teaching me lessons on patience. Instructing me to trust my first mind. Coaching me to be a better mother. All while loving me unconditionally as I tried to figure out how to be the best version of myself for you. After you were born, I still thought I could have it all. The career, the house, the perfect family. I soon realized that raising a Black Son would require me to assess what was truly important. I could not in good conscience focus my energy on building a career when there may be a chance that you could be taken from my life by someone who saw you as anything other than a child of God. I stepped back (in my career) to ensure all of my "extra" time could be spent with my family. I sacrificed for you so I would have no regrets if something out of my control ever happened to you. This has been one of the best decisions I have made since you were born.

I admire your curiosity, sense of humor and how loving you are. I pray these character traits follow you into adulthood. At times in your life you will experience disappointment, feel discouraged or just downright sad. I want you to know this is common and everyone feels this way at times. What ultimately matters is your bounce back. You cannot control what happens to you, but you can control how you react to the situation.

Before I close, let me share some advice I hope you find helpful throughout your life:

- *Always remember to connect with people on a human level; everyone has a story, and everyone matters.*
- *Help lift people up by working to improve their condition; however, they will need to fight to improve themselves.*
- *People will make assumptions about who you are without ever having a conversation with you. They may even go as far as to try an assume agency over you, your body or both. Remember to advocate for yourself as you know what is best for you.*
- *Always expect the best out of yourself, not the worst. And... promise Mommy as you get older, you will not ever let anyone diminish your light.*

Everything I have ever done and ever will do will be from a place of love.

Love Always...Mommy

A Note to My Black Son Anthony, My Little Tony…

On Nina Simone's, Black Gold album, she ministers a song for the souls of Black Youth, "To Be Young, Gifted and Black." These words are a catalyst for the pride and the joy found in realizing the pricelessness of walking in your true identity. You, my Son, personify this chorus. You are young. You are gifted. You are unapologetically Black.

*My Son, you are young. Being young will not stop you. It will not silence you. It will not keep you from accomplishing great things NOW! The Bible tells us in **Jeremiah 1:7** (NIV), "…Do not say, 'I am too young.' You must go to everyone I send you to say whatever I command you." Being young and being sent by God commands an honor and respect that this world does not dictate. There is knowing beyond your years housed in your heart. Trust the words God gives you in your youth. Deny fear any stolen territory and SPEAK! Youth, though temporary, is a gift and a treasure. Invest it with God's guidance.*

*My Son, you are gifted! Being gifted will not derail you. It will not sidetrack you. Your gifts will propel you forward and open doors that no Man could shut. The gift must be surrendered and submitted to the Giver. The word of God reminds us that, "Every good and perfect gift is from above." (**James 1:17, NIV**) That verse goes on to remind us that God does not change, nor does He change His mind about the gift that He has entrusted to you. He stitched your gifts together with your life. Use your gift. Never let others use you to get your gift. Multiply your gifts with practice, productive struggle and purpose. Your life is God's art. Giftedness is never revoked, so entrust the Lord with the fruits of the evidence of the masterpiece of His that you are.*

My Son, you are unapologetically Black. Your hair curls with the inescapable influence of your ancestors. Your voice quickens with the melodic rhythms that no doubt hailed from the shores of Africa. As your voice deepens and you grow taller you have to know that it is not your assignment to straighten the crooked paths that make others fear you simply because you exist in Black brilliance. This world will try to reduce you to a statistic, a number, or a hashtag. I speak the truth of who you are over you today and I pray your heart receives this declaration. You are pure genius and unadulterated joy. You are resilience brushed with defiance. You are a creative force that rebels against the status quo. You build up others. You tear down oppression. Your life teaches the infiniteness of God's possibilities. You are empowered not endangered. You are young. You are gifted. You are Black, and baby, that makes you blessed. I am so grateful God chose you to be my Son. Live freely in Christ! I love you, always.

Love Always…Mommy

Photo By: Anita Shultz (Anita Louise Photography)

A Note to My Black Son Carlos, My Pumpkin...

Words cannot express how much I love you. You are the best Son I could have ever asked for and you are exactly what I needed in my life. You are strong, brilliant, hilarious and thoughtful. Do not allow this world to change who you are. Regardless of what goes on around you, continue to be the leader you have always been and know that I will always be here to support you in whatever you do.

Love Always...Mommy

A Note to My Black Son Anthony…

My love for you has no boundaries!! I have been in awe that God would bless me with someone as special as you. Being your Mom has been a privilege, honor and stressful all at once. I feel blessed and honored because of the JOY you have given me! I have experienced anxiety and stress because of the world we live in!

All through your childhood and as an adult, I have tried to speak positivity, life and love into the words I say to you daily. There was a phrase I would always say, "Be mindful of the decisions that you make, they can control your destiny." I am proud to say you listened (maybe not all the time), but you were always open to agree to disagree if we did not come to an understanding.

Know that I am so proud of the man you have become, and feel anxiety anticipating and watching all your dreams come true, through all of your hard work and determination.

Remember you are capable of GREATNESS!!

Love Always…Mom

A Note to My Black Son Reggie…

This world is cruel, and it can make you feel that you are unworthy, but I am here to tell you that you ARE more than worthy. You are phenomenally made by your parents and by God.

Though you need to be careful as you navigate through life because of racism and fear, walk proud! I know some day you might feel defeated, hold your head up and be strong!

Being your Mom has been one of my most special accomplishments in life. I worry about you when you are not near, but trust that God will cover you.

Know that I am and always will be proud of the young man you have grown into. Be fearless, faithful and forever the King that you are…

Love Always…Mom

A Note to My Black Son Jay...

You are amazing, you are smart, and whatever stands in your way, you jump over! I love and admire you for that. I pray that you hold your head high with complete humbleness in everything you do, love in your actions, compassion in your thoughts, and faith in your heart. With the confidence of knowing that being a Black Man you can accomplish anything you want, overcome any barriers that are in your way, and create your own unique path of greatness, no matter who tells you that you cannot or the negativity that comes your way. Soar high, spread your wings, and fly to great heights.

Love Always...Mommy

Photo By: Rudy (The Cleveland Gallery)

A Note to My Black Son Raymond, My Sweet Pea…

Where do I even start?! I remember just having you the summer of my last year at OSU and me still trying to figure out how was I going to do it. Here I am in Columbus with no family well (I really just wanted my Mother). I remember my Mom saying just come back home and my response was naw, my degree is about to say THE Ohio State University. It was one of those situations that you learn how to adapt and keep it moving without making any excuses. There were times I had you in class with me because I just did not have anywhere for you to go. But can we say I got that degree and you were only 6-months-old. I felt like in the process we were going together, and I was still trying to figure this thing called "Mom" out. What I have noticed being a Mom is how you define it and things you do to make the best for your child. There were times that I was okay with making you think the world was so perfect, but as you got older I noticed that I am raising a Black Man and it was time for me to stop shielding the truth from you.

I leave with some positive ideas based on the poem "Hey, Black Child" by Countee Cullen:

❖ *You are strong; REALLY strong*
❖ *You can do what you want to do; all you have to do is TRY*

Yes, you Raymond you are STRONG and you CAN DO WHAT YOU WANT TO DO as long as you TRY and NOT GIVE UP.

Love Always…Mommy

Photo By: Ryan Harris (RH Imagery Capturing)

A Note to My Black Sons Samuel and Elijah,

God formed you both in my womb, so you are undoubtedly amazing! You two were fearfully and wonderfully made by Him. God had you in mind and had you in mind specifically for me! You both entered the world uniquely, yet both decided to enter with quite the bang! (that almost took Mommy's life, yet I have no regrets!) I feel so blessed to have been chosen to be responsible for such beautiful Black beings. Samuel and Elijah, there is a saying: "I would give you the world if I could". There was a time I may have felt that way, but now I see the world as no prize at all. Unfortunately, you guys must live in a world that has been turned completely upside down. In fact, you Boys are the prize, given to the world.

Please be better, think better, talk better, do better than this world. Rise above the hate, the injustices, and the prejudices. Always remember that you Boys are children of God, therefore you are royalty! No matter what ANYONE says, you are NOT to be labeled as anything outside of amazing, beautiful, intelligent, charismatic, important, valuable, special, strong, influential, talented, bright, remarkable, educated, and promising, just to name a few. You both are loved in a way I cannot even express with words. Sam and Eli, I am proud of you two; I know that you will continue to make us proud. Stand TALL, stand STRONG, and stand BOLDLY! Remember, always let your light shine bright, despite the world trying to dim it. I love you both to the heavens and back!

Love Always…Mommy

A Note to My Black Son Brandon...

The time is NOW! Not tomorrow, or the next day...but NOW...live the dream, write the book, run the race... whatever it is do it NOW! Every morning are new mercies, a new day, a new year, a new beginning. Do not waste it thinking about time gone by (because it is not lost, we just did not take full advantage of it)...take full advantage of THIS moment of NOW and be AMAZING!

Give notice and step into your destiny. It is time...you have been at this mountain long enough... now it is time for you to move into what has been designed and waiting for you all along!

And as you move into your rightful position in life, resolve that no longer will you be anyone other than you. Resolve that you will not dim your light because they forgot their sunglasses. Do not hide your light or your power; quiet those internal and external voices that will say "Who are you to be" ... (fill in the blank), and remember "Who you are"!

Use the weapons that have been imparted in you before the beginning of time. The power that God has given you, your voice. I AM...two of the most POWERFUL words...I AM...can either create or destroy...build up or tear down...we speak it audibly or internally...either way we have created what we see in our lives. And in doing so, always know that You are worthy. You are beautiful. You are enough. You lack nothing...because You Are. Do not shrink because there is GREATNESS in you!

Love Always...Mommie

A Note to My Black Son Kristian, My Do Butt...

To my only Son...at first, I was like no this cannot be right; then I was like okay it is me and him against the world. Dilating 2 cm at 19 weeks, being put on bedrest the rest of my pregnancy; yes, these last 7-months have been nothing but blessings. Me watching you grow from 29-weeks at 3lb, 13 oz., 16.5 in; 40 days in the hospital without me leaving your side or me making the sacrifice to start work 2-weeks after your birth to make sure we were all set before you came home.

You are truly my little soldier; it still amazes me that I am your mother, but I would not have it any other way! I am here to tell you, as well as, teach you that you can be ANYTHING you want to be as long as you put God first and believe in yourself. You may get kicked down in life or things might not go your way but, NEVER give up. I will always have your back no matter what. I am raising a young, Black King who will soon be someone's Doctor, Lawyer, Husband and Father.

Love Always...Mommy

Photo By: Raquel Reyes

A Note to My Black Son Aden, My Sweet Pea…

Nothing in the world could have prepared me for your love that I never knew I desperately needed. Your patience has taught me to remain calm in the toughest storms. Your kindness has taught me to never take for granted a generous gesture. Your love has taught me what true love is as I struggled with who I was internally. As a young, first time Mother, I brought you into this world filled with so much optimism and hope but what you did not see was my fear. "Was I capable of raising a Black Son in this world? Did I make the right decision to bring you into this world? Will I become another statistic?" Those were my thoughts as I looked in your beautiful, brown face every day for a year of your life as I battled with postpartum depression. In the midst of my lack of confidence, you gave me strength and wiped my tears not even understanding the internal struggle I was going through. It was then I knew that we were meant to be and that I made the right decision. It was then that I felt and understood what real love is. It was then that I knew we would be just fine on this life journey together. As children, we remember our parents as the superhero in our story called life, however, Aden you were my superhero. I was drowning in life and somehow just a simple smile from you would pick me up during the roughest times. There were times I questioned my own life and it was as if God was sending me a message through you to not give up. No matter how much you grow or how big you become, you will always be my baby…MY SUPERHERO. Always remember you are amazing, your intelligence and brilliance is out of this world and your love is more than I could have ever imagined. Thank you for saving me.

Love Always… Mommy

Photo By: Made by Glyde

A Note to My Black Son Braydon, My Sweet Pea…

Braydon, I thank God for choosing me to be your mother. You made me a mother in the middle of a scary pandemic. These past few months have been a rollercoaster, but I would not trade one moment of this journey for anything. Braydon, you refused to show your face for the entire nine months but boy was it worth the wait. I have never known a love like the one I felt the first time I looked into your big, beautiful eyes. Your dimpled smile and infectious laugh melt my heart. You are truly evidence of God's unmerited love for me.

I know that as you grow, there will be struggles, but please know Braydon that just like God our Heavenly Father, Momma will ALWAYS be there, and you can ALWAYS count on me. In due time, there will be some tough conversations that we will and must have simply because the world fears your beautiful, brown skin, and Momma is ready to ensure that you are fully equipped to take your rightful place in this world.

No matter what the world tells you, Momma needs you to know that you are loved, you are blessed, you are favored, and you are purposed. Momma needs you to know that with God's help you can do whatever you want to do and be whoever you want to be in this world.
Proverbs 16:7 (NKJV) *states, "When a man's ways please the Lord, He makes even his enemies be at peace with him." With God, you are destined for greatness my Son. It is the joy of my life to watch you grow into the Man that God has already ordained that you be. I count it an honor to be assigned the task of raising a King and with God, I know I will not fail. I love you more than words can convey. Braydon be assured that Momma will work every day to make sure that her love will forever be on full display.*

Love Always…Momma

A Note to My Black Son Jaylin…

Premature…that is how your arrival was labeled. I did not get to hold you because they rushed you away so soon. You were so tiny and bruised up. But Boy, you were mighty strong inside of that fragile, glass box. It was the moment I held you that I realized I was the mother to a brave child!

Jaylin, I want you to know, I will always love you and as you grow older, you will face many obstacles in life; we live in a very cruel world. Stay strong, be confident and always do your best! If you do not remember anything else Jay, remember that there is power in prayer.

Love Always…Mommy

A Note to My Black Son Michael, My Boots…

To my son, my baby whom I love dearly. The blessing of your life has taught me a new purpose for mine. The glow of your eyes and sound of your voice illuminates even the darkest of days. You have so much to give to this world and so much joy inside. I hope that your love for exploration and learning never ends.

My prayer for you is to never give up. That your empathy, compassion and understanding are immeasurable; that your health remains; that God guides me to protect you; that your love is endless; that you always find safety and love from your family.

Always be courageous and bold. Never dim your light. Remain true to yourself and hold tight to honesty and humility. I am excited to see your contributions to our community. You are destined to be so much more than anyone can imagine. I love you beyond the bounds and ties of time and space. You are MY Black Son, my baby.

Love Always…Mommy

Photo By: Loreal Holt (Photos by Loreal Diane)

A Note to My Black Son Cameron…

You have been the perfect gift from God. I am in awe of your heart, your faith, your work ethic, your strength, your love of family and every bit of what makes you who you are. I have been nothing BUT proud of you, and it has been a joy to watch you grow. You are one of the two great accomplishments in my life. I will always be your biggest fan, supporter, confidant and truth teller.

You were taught that this world is far from perfect and far from fair and that often you would be initially judged just by the color of your skin. As a Black Man, you must be smarter, stronger and work twice as hard to reach your goals and to acquire half of what the others have. And you have always done exactly what was required of you and more.

When your father passed, I was so worried that you would lose your way, because he was such a major influence in your life. But because of the wisdom your father had already provided, your faith in God and the village of men that He strategically placed in your life, your path has been lit with opportunity and blessings; I thank God for that daily. You may not have taken the desired road but your journey thus far (struggles and all) has been inspiring, and I am sure there are bigger and better things to come. I cannot wait to see all the places this expedition takes you.

Continue to reach for the stars and rely on your relationship with God; He will always take care of you. And I will continue to do my part as your Mother and pray for mercy and grace over your life, that you stay rooted in faith, that you have continued health and safety (from enemies known and unknown).

GOOD BETTER BEST, NEVER EVER REST, UNTIL YOUR GOOD IS BETTER, AND YOUR BETTER IS BEST!

Love always…Mommy

A note to my Black Son Jackson, My Blessing….

I am writing you this note on the verge of civil unrest in our country as yet another Black Man has made national headline news as he was the victim of police brutality. This time, his name is Jacob Blake. When I learned that his 3 Sons were in the car and witnessed him get shot seven times in the back, all I could do was go to your room and lay hands over you and pray over you with tears in my eyes as you slept.

I am writing you this note after the passing of Chadwick Boseman, T'Challa our Black Panther King. Mr. Boseman was a perfect example of a Man of astute character that I envision for your life. Despite his own trials and physical pain, he gave the world powerful examples of our Black excellence through his craft! You my beloved Son, are Black excellence! You my beloved Son are blessed and highly favored by the Most High! Like Chadwick, I hope the ancestors are proud when they welcome you to the ancestral realm.

When I was pregnant with you, God assured me that you would be blessed! Seriously! There was a time early on in my pregnancy that there was a possibility that we were going to lose you. I laid in that cold hospital room and I prayed to God and I firmly believe that God spoke to me as clear as day and said, "Your SON will be blessed!" We did not know your sex at that time, but a calm came over me and I was reassured that everything would be fine. All of the other turmoil that I had endured or would experience during the duration of my pregnancy no longer bothered me, because I was assured by God's promise that your life would be blessed! The name Jackson means, "God has favored". I did not know this until you were 9 years old, but it makes perfect sense!

And Kinfolk, despite our hardships, your life has been blessed and God has showed favor over your life! Your life has definitely been a blessing for my life as well! You are my reason for breathing. Every sacrifice is worth it! I love you unconditionally! There is absolutely nothing that can make me not love, support, or sacrifice on your behalf!

You are a leader. You are such a good friend. You are so intelligent! You are a great athlete. You are funny, honest and consider other's feelings. You are a proud Black Boy that will grow up to be a proud Black Man. You are already a Man of your word and proven to be a Man of good character and honor. Always remember, that despite what the world thinks of you or what the world throws at you; YOU ARE BLESSED! You are a child of the Most High! I gave you a strong name for a reason. You have Croley, Bassey and Campbell blood flowing through your veins and Mommy loves you more than life! I am so proud of you Jackson!

Love Always…Mommy (your biggest fan!)

A Note to My Black Son Harlan, My 'Chief'…

My sweet, hilarious, intelligent, loving and loyal SONshine…you have been such a blessing to me. I get choked up just at the thought of you and how much I love you. From the time that you were very young you stole the hearts of everyone you encountered; that stands true today. You have an undeniable presence that says, "Hello, I am here!" I absolutely love that about you. You have a way of demanding attention (and respect) which is partially how you earned the nickname 'Chief'.

Your ever present leadership qualities have been with you your whole life. I recall attending a parent-teacher conference for you in 2nd grade at your new school. The teacher said, "Everyone wants to be wherever Harlan is." I knew then that I had to keep a close eye on you. ☺

As parents, we pour into our children all of the life lessons we can possibly think of to ensure we are giving them all the tools they need to be a successful member of society with sound morals and values. As I watch you interact with your friends, family, church family, strangers and during professional settings, I am very pleased and blown away each time. When you gave your acceptance speech after receiving the Young Man of the Year Award at church, I remember sitting there in awe…amazed at your words, your passion and your delivery as tears streamed down my face. I was soooo proud of you but mostly I felt eternally grateful that God chose ME to be YOUR Mother! I remember asking what I did to be given such an honor?

As I reflect on your life, your greatness, your accomplishments and even in anticipation of what is to come, I cannot help but to feel frightened and saddened of what could come. As the Mother of a Black Son, I pray in a different way than I pray for your sister. When you leave the house I pray to God that He returns you home safely and that you do not encounter a police officer who is threatened by you due to the color of your skin, your stature or even your intelligence. When you first started hanging out independently (and 'til this day), I would say to you, "BE SAFE, BE SMART, HAVE FUN…in that order". The fact that I feel compelled to speak those words to you indicates that the world still needs a lot of love, prayer and compassion.

So as you go about each day, remember to pray and remember the words from some of the affirmations you spoke as a kid and more recent ones shared…YOU ARE THE BADDEST DUDE ON THE PLANET! YOU ARE BRAVER THAN YOU BELIEVE, STRONGER THAN YOU SEEM AND SMARTER THAN YOU THINK, and LOVED MORE THAN YOU KNOW! I love you Son.

Love Always…Ma Dukes

A Note to My Black Son Jaden...

In a world designed to keep you down, know that I will always hold you up. In a world where your melanated skin is seen as a threat, understand that your skin tone makes you royalty. Your skin tone is not a threat, but you my Son, are a threat to this world. Your greatness, your strength, and your intellectual abilities are the real threat; because those things are the qualities that make you superior. No matter what you are told, or what may be done to you, remember that greatness runs through your veins and embodies your genetic makeup. You are a King! Speak with conviction, smile with confidence, and walk with pride; be a fearless leader, but lead with love and respect. Embrace your roots, because they are the basis of your foundation, and there is nothing stronger. My Black Son Jaden, you are blessed beyond measure, and know that as long as I can breathe, I will support you and protect you. No matter the circumstance, never feel that you are alone, because even if I cannot physically be there, you are still covered by the blood of Jesus. So, fly high My Black Son Jaden, and take advantage of every opportunity given. Believe in your dreams and conquer every goal that you set. My Kind, Black Son, you are worthy, and you can do anything your heart desires.

Love Always...Mom

A Note to My Black Son Jordan…

You are Great! Greatness created you, Greatness lives within you. Greater is He that is within you. You have purpose. You are destined for greatness.

You are loved! You were created in love and through love. For God so loved the world that He gave his only begotten son. That is love. **John 3:16**

Dream Big! Be all you can be. Follow your dreams and passions. For He knows the plans He has for you. Plans to prosper and not harm, to give you hope for the future. Aim high in your aspirations reach for the universe. **Jeremiah 29:11**

Be knowledgeable. Seek higher understanding. Know all you can learn; learning is a continuous process. An Idle mind is a mind of the enemy. Acknowledge flaws and weaknesses, improve upon them. Build on your strengths and stand firm on the promises of the Most High.

Stay strong my Black Son. Breathe. As a Black Man you will face many trials and tribulations of hatred, deceit and persecution but please do not let it distract you. Control you only. Many will push you to weep, acknowledge your pain and grow through it. God has planted a seed in you to be a vessel. Through challenge comes grace. You are a child of a King. Therefore, you are a King. Always stand aplomb with your head up, look everyone in the eye and keep a firm handshake. You can do all things through Christ, who strengthens you. **Philippians 4:13**

You are a unique creation, created to do wonderful things.

Operate in purpose on purpose at all times.

Always do well in all you do.

No matter where you are, you can always grow.

Make wise choices; stay aware.

Be confident in who you are.

Be authentic; be you unapologetically.

These are words of encouragement and development grow through it, lean on it, love always and stand on the promises of our Creator. You have a blessing over your life. The mission and vision have been set operate in it. You are your own Brand. Stand on your integrity. Always remember **Who** *you are and* **Whose** *you are. Show light-Jordan Kent Birch.*

Love Always…Mommy Danielle M. Birch

Black Mom & Baby Illustration By: Rodney Potts

A Note to My Black Sons Benjamin & Jacob, My Big Ben and Small Fry…

Boys it has been such a joy to be called your Mom. I never even imagined myself being a Mother, let alone the Mother of two amazing boys like you. I was 30 and 34 when you boys were born, and I was petrified! I had obtained multiple degrees, I was married, had all types of professional savvy, but I still was not sure if I would make the cut as a Mother. The world was becoming such a scary place, filled with hatred and so much uncertainty, I did not know if I would be able to keep you safe. But let me tell you boys, the moment I held you in my arms I knew that I was going to fiercely protect you with every fiber of my being. I knew that I was going to be a part of every step, every moment, every laugh and every tear as long as there was breath in my body. That is exactly what I have done. I cannot believe we have moved from learning to walk and talk to learning to drive, playing sports and working in the family business. Looking back, I thought there would be more time with my baby boys, but here we are. You two are becoming such outstanding young men, you WILL change the world.

As you move into teenagers and young adulthood there are just a few things I want my two boys to hear from their Mother. First, know that you are gifted, intelligent and strong boys. Unfortunately, there are some who will make assumptions about you and your abilities simply based on the fact that you are young Black Boys. Although I wish that I could protect you from these people, I know that when those times come you will boldly look racism and bias in the face and be unapologetically you! Second, there will be times when things get really hard in your life and the battle seems all uphill. Never forget that you boys were both premature babies born with the odds against you and you fought to survive. You fought to live. When you feel like you cannot win the fight, I want you to reach deep inside and channel that same will to thrive that brought you home with no complications and has sustained you ever since. Remember what is in your names. Finally, know that your lives mean something and you are here for a reason. Live in such a way that someone else's life is enriched because you were a part of it. Remember that money, clothes and possessions come and go, but your true legacy will be in the lives you touched while you were here. That sons, is your God ordained destiny: to change the world we live in, and I have no doubt you will do just that.

So, when I am no longer physically here with you, know that nothing has meant more to me than being your Mom. And when you close your eyes you will hear me singing the words from the Robert Munsch book…" I'll love you forever, I'll like you for always…" My love for you boys transcends all space and time, forever and ever my babies you will be.

Love Always…Momma

Photo By: Natasha Herbert Photography

A Note to My Black Son Daniel…

"When, I wake up before I put on my makeup. I say a little prayer for you" Aretha Franklin

Being your mother has been my greatest joy. When you were born, you spent eight days in the NICU. We were alone. I was afraid. All the nurses and doctors said, "If you have to have a baby in the NICU, Daniel is the baby you want!" You suckled and were breathing on your own. I prayed that Allah would provide me ease through this hardship. Since then, it has been you and me against the world.

My love for you is consistently opposed by my fears for you. You are an African American, Muslim, Gay, male living, growing and thriving in America. Every time you leave our home, I am praying that the world sees the charismatic, intellectual you are and not act on the fear your skin ignites in them consciously or subconsciously. I am relieved every day you return home unscathed. I pray that the invisible bruises of institutionalized racism do not impact your spirit. I pray that you continue to find more joy than sorrow in this life. I pray you find a partner and live happily ever after. I pray your children; my grandchildren enjoy greater acceptance because your generation's vigilant pursuit of equality. I apologize for my generation's complicit attitude and reluctance to pursue equality through any means necessary because of fear.

I know as the parent I am supposed to be the teacher and you the learner. Well, do not tell anyone but you have always been smarter than me. I remember teaching you to play chess and within a week you beat me at opportunity. My learning from you is so much deeper than chess. 2020 has been a year of great challenge. You did not tell me you were participating in the protests. Yet, when you return, I realized you actionized life lessons, I have tried to imprint in your consciousness. The lessons you applied to the protest I know you will apply in life. Your actions brought me peace. Son be great! Do not let anyone dim your light!

Love Always…Mom

A Note to My Black Sons My <u>Melly-Pell</u> and <u>Loopy</u>...

I cannot say enough that I am so proud to be your Mom. Through all that we three have had to survive, we still made it and stuck like glue. We are our own "Big Three." We are in sad times but you both have survived and thrived.

Melly-Pell, my oldest Son, my longest companion: You are my love, my sweet boy. Kind and considerate to a fault. I love that you are willingly selfless, that you give, and give and you never expect anything in return. You are a wonderful Father and your daughters are so blessed to be able to call you "Daddy." You love for them is relentless, your desire for their best is above even your own well-being. You are a wonderful example of how, sacrifice and perseverance will pay off in the long run. Even when you fall, you manage to get up and always smile. Not a fake I am trying smile, but a real genuine "I know that God has me and that everything will be alright" smile. I am overwhelmed by your love and the wisdom you have spoken to me and so many others. I could have never imagined your infinite wisdom. I pray that all you desire and work so hard to achieve, you get. I pray that your health will not fail you and your heart will not faint. I pray that you will always know that I have your back and I am pulling for your winning season. My love for you will always be...Love you always and forever with my entire heart.

Love Always...Mommy

Loopy, my youngest Son, and little "old Man": You are my smart and brassy Boy. You and I have endured some very rough patches brought on by my immature decisions. You never held it against me even when, I confessed and blamed myself. You always are willing to forgive and move on; showing me that forgiveness is better. You continue to grow as a Man and now, a Father. Your smile is infectious, and your talents are immeasurable. I have no doubt that you will achieve everything you set your mind to. In recently becoming a Father to a smart and brassy Boy, it is fun and refreshing to watch you work. Your love for him is so wonderful to see and his crazy love for you is amazing. I marvel at you as a Father because you always said you would never have children; God thought different. You are a beautiful human being and everyone who comes in contact with you is impressed and imprinted by your being and energy. Although you did not achieve some of your childhood dreams, you pressed on into your very bright future. I love you Son, always will, forever and forever even before you got here.

Love Always...Ma

A Note to My Black Sons P.J. and Mike, My Heartbeats….

As I write this letter, you two have just turned 30 and 27 and ironically, I was 27 when I had you P.J. and 30 when I birthed you Michael James. P.J., I remember as you approached adulthood, I began to call you Paul and you so abruptly turned your head and asked me if I was crazy. You then said, "Ma, don't call me that. People who are close to me call me P.J." Well excuse me, eldest Son of mine. Mike, you on the other hand were called Michael James as though both names represented you. Later, I fell into the mode of Mike Mike to now most recently, Mike.

I want both of you to know how enormously proud I am of all your accomplishments and what is represented by the signature of your name. You carry my DNA, my grit and tenacity and most of all my grind. You two are so different, but just like Mommy in so many ways. P.J., I am convinced you get your calmness from Mar Mar which in my eyes sometimes comes across as a nonchalant mood. You know how I check you when you seem unbothered and not as dramatic as I. On the other hand, Mike you have taken my sarcasm to an entirely different level (also known as "throwing shade").

There is not a day or night that passes where I do not whisper a special prayer for my Black Sons. I get nervous even now for your safety. Walking while BLACK, standing while BLACK, driving while BLACK and even succeeding while BLACK…the list goes on. I pray that you two continue to be great Dads in the eyes of Nana's babies. They deserve everything you were afforded and more. I taught you sacrifice, if nothing else, and what it means to always say "I Love You". I expect you to treat women with dignity and pride and always have a visual of how you wanted Mommy to be treated. You both have supported me, loved me and taken care of me as I always hoped you would. People talk about the bond between Mother and Son, but I know firsthand times 2. I charge you to always hold each other accountable. You are brothers first and brothers for life.

Love Always…Mommy

A Note to My Black Sons Ameer, My Perfect Prince & Kanaan, My Promised Child…

I did not know what to write, or that I <u>would even</u> write but at 4:45 am on a Tuesday morning, a few days before this is due as you Kanaan sleep with your feet kicking me and Ameer your asleep in your room, God wakes me to write these words. My prayer is that these words will bless you and someone else.

I am thankful for you. I cried when the sonogram technician said "and there is his penis" (both times). There are days that I am terrified for you. As Black Boys that will be Men who love God, I pray that you will be Men that show compassion, kindness, grace, mercy, valor, ethics, morals, integrity, generosity, wisdom, respect, strength (physical, mental, and emotional), vulnerability (when appropriate), humility, and love of self and others. I know your path will not be an easy one. You will be judged by your skin color, your hair texture and choice, your tone or lack of and those special qualities that are unique to you that most will not take the time to understand. However, you are Black, Negro, African American Boys that will be Men. You were the first on this planet. You come from the DNA of a woman that was blessed to create every variation of "Man" on this planet. That one truth is power and knowledge. Acknowledge, accept and build upon the greatness of your DNA, your ancestors and your history. Learn it, use it and create a powerful legacy of those qualities I stated above and wealth. I empower you, pray for you and implore you to utilize the strength of our past to forge a future that will diminish your struggles, place favor in your path, create blessed relationships, powerful allies and provide you with peace, joy and understanding of your worth!

I may have been well intentioned but I have not always made the right decisions. There will be days where you do not make the right choice. I ask that you question yourself, "How will the choice I make impact others?" This question does not make you selfless. However, does not asking the questions make you selfish? How will eating this last chocolate cookie affect my family? Did Mommy or my Sisters get one? Will it improve my health? Have I had enough? Will this cause someone else harm or cause me harm? You see the foundational question leads to other questions which leads to other questions. The choice to eat the chocolate chip cookie can be easy or difficult. Allow the original question to serve as a guide: an internal measure as your knowledge, heart and self-worth mold you into the Great Black Man, God's original creation, that He has called you to be. I love you with infinite Magic Kisses!

Love Always…Mommy

A Note to My Black Son Ellis Hicks, My Son-Shine…

I write this letter to you with a heavy heart, hoping to find the words to inspire you (and myself), but this year 2020 has just taken such a heavy toll on everyone. Our spirits and emotions are drained. A once in a lifetime global pandemic is happening, with no end in sight. We still have to watch the killing of unarmed Black Men and Women, with no justice in sight. Enough is ENOUGH! Black Lives Matter! Always have and always will! For me your Black Life Matters immensely! I want to see your Black Life thrive and grow. Make an impact in the world and pave the way for future generations of Black Lives. That is my role as your Mother. Thankfully, it is not all doom and gloom. There is joy in the world, because there is more good in the world than bad and I want you to remember You are love and light. There is joy in your laughter. There is kindness and empathy in your heart. There is understanding, compassion and intelligence in your mind. Always remember the energy that you put out, is the energy that you get back. Never forget to speak up for yourself and for others who are not able to speak up for themselves. Know that I love you and want nothing but the best for you. Your Journey will be very different than mine, but I want you to enjoy it. Learn from every moment, live your life to the fullest. You will soon begin the next chapter of your life off to college. The world is about open up for you and all that I have written here will make sense to you.

Love Always…Mom (Ericka Hicks)

A Note to My Black Sons Donovan (Don-Don) & Owen (OJ)…

My love for you will never waiver. You can always and forever count on me being by your side. The joy that it brings me to watch you two growing up makes my heart full. Each day, you will be challenged within yourself and by society. I hope that the guidance and wisdom that I provide you will make each life choice a blessing. The learning experiences that you have, good and bad, will help mold you in becoming the best person possible. Some will see you as a threat and not as the wonderful life you are. Do not let the ignorance taught to some people dim your light. Society will try to put you in a box but think bigger. As you both become contributing members to society always remember…You are important. You are smart. You are loved. You are most importantly God's Child. You are NOT a threat.

Love always…Mom

A Note to My Black Son Eric…

ERIC, as I look at the picture I found of us when you were 3 months old, I remember the dreams that I had for you. When you were born, you were my EVERYTHING. I was only 23 years old and had no idea where life would take us, but one thing I knew was that I would love and take care of you the best that I could. Because of you, I found my voice; because of you, I found my strength; because of you, I understood what it meant to love and be loved unconditionally on Earth.

I learned so much from you. You were my ride or die buddy. I took you everywhere and did not trust too many people with my precious baby, LOL! If you could not come, then, I was not going to go. We have been through so much.

As you grew, I realized more and more the precious gift that God had given me. I realized as a Black Boy, you would encounter many challenges through your journey in life. I tried to expose you to as many experiences as I could. I made many mistakes along the way but one thing that never wavered was my love for you. Now that you are a Man, I realize the importance of my role in your life. God also had me realize the importance of releasing you to live your life.

You are very smart and very funny…a true comedian. I love being around you and I am proud of the man you have become. I pray for you daily. I pray for your spiritual development, mental strength, and physical health. I pray for God's protection for you every day of your life. I pray for my Black Son, I love you, ERIC.

Love Always…Mom

A Note to My Black Son Chris...

Chris, I can remember when you were 5 years old and we had to have "The Talk." You were in kindergarten and you came home crying because the other kids did not want to play with you. I had to then tell you that the world is not fair. That sometimes you will be treated unjustly. I had to tell you that simply because of the color of your skin people will treat you differently. I told you that the people who are supposed to protect and serve may hurt you because of the color of your skin. And that is why I pray for you every single day. When I wake up in the morning, I ask for God to put a hedge of protection around you. It is unfortunate but that is the conversation that we had to have.

And now or 20 years later, we are in the same place. I pray for you every single day. When I see on the news that a young Black Man has been shot and killed. I have to pause for a moment and praise God that it is not you and pick up the phone to call or text you to ensure that you are okay. Now I have put you in God's hands. I ask Him to put His hedge of protection around you; bless your comings and goings.

I thank God that you have turned out to be the Man that you are today. I am so proud of you. And you are the joy of my life and I love you with all my heart.

Love Always...Mom

Photo By: Alvin Smith

A Note to My Black Son Mason aka Funnyface….

The moment you arrived, I was so relieved, and I knew you would be perfect. You decided I needed to slow down to grow you, so I was on bedrest for 4 months. You decided I needed to grow you a couple extra days, so you were late. You decided you wanted to make a grand entrance, so you waited out the 18 hours of labor and came by C-section. But again, you were perfect. A splendid mix of your father and me. From that point on you have done things your own way. Your way was not always the conventional way and it would later be labeled: Autism is the label that was used. But despite that, you overcame all obstacles. Your ability to find joy every day is amazing. You care so deeply and show love in many ways. I pray that the world was more like you. Unfortunately, I know all too well that it is not. I wish I could shield you and protect from this harsh world forever. I pray that you will continue to find joy and love from here on out.

I pray the world will know the amazing artist you are. It is hard to navigate this world when you do things so differently, but there are many things that have a similar language like Art. One of my fondest memories is of you coming home from seeing "Finding Nemo" and I asked you how the movie was, and you just ran to your room. Several minutes went by and you returned with a picture detailing the movie. You have always used your art to express yourself even when you cannot find the words. You also taught yourself to play "Happy Birthday" to your younger sister on your big cousin's guitar after having never picked one up. You played songs by ear on a small keyboard you had from younger years. Your dad continues to upgrade your keyboards and you find ways daily to express yourself.

You never cease to amaze. I hope you continue to learn from the wonderful example your father has set. You will be King one day, and I hope you can lead your family with the strength, wisdom, and selflessness your father has led us with. I hope that you find a love that is beyond understanding. I pray that you bring beautiful children in the world and they bring you as much joy as you have brought your Father and I.

*I always hope that you know how much you are loved. Our world would not be the same if you had never entered it. You are very special Son and I cherish all the memories I have with you and will continue to have. I pray for as much time as the Lord will allow to continue to be blessed with love. You will always be our **Funnyface** and **Squeak-a-Deek**. We love you so much and would give you the world if we could.*

Love Always…Mom

A Note to My Black Son My Handsome Junior, My Baby...

I want you to know the you are God's child. You will conquer everything that comes against you. You will be a Black, educated, successful and intelligent young man one day. I want to remind you that regardless of the skin you and your Black Brothers and friends all wear, you ALL are beautiful in the eyes of our Creator and I am proud of you. I love you son, always!

Love Always...Mommy

A Note to My Black Sons Jake and Josh...

Life is nothing but a journey. And your journey will be transitory. While the days may seem long, everyone's years on Earth are very short. And in that very short time, my prayer is that you use your gifts and talents to have an impact. When you leave this world, I hope that it will be a much better place because of the talents that you have so generously shared with others.

Throughout the years, I helped you in developing your talents so that you would have a strong foundation, and your life would have great meaning. Many did not understand why I worked so hard to expose you to so many different things. As you continue to grow, I encourage you to unapologetically accept your unique God given abilities. Always plug into your gifts and talents, and never check out. Look at the things you are naturally good at, and naturally gravitate towards. Listen to the things other people confirm about you that has made an impact on their life. Think about the things you do that give you a sense of happiness and fulfillment. Embrace and fight for every opportunity to explore new things. Be diligent in improving your talents, so that others will see your passion, progress and desire for self-improvement. Work hard to evolve your gifts and talents, because ten years from now they will not be the same as they are today. And always remember to adopt the perspective of a true student who is not afraid to ask questions, because you know practice makes perfect. If you do not practice your gifts and talents in different ways, you will never know where your journey may have led you.

Your gifts and talents are meant for you to enjoy, but also for you to share with those less fortunate than you. Build others up and bring them along as you transition through life. Like I taught you, do not be afraid to carry the heavy load and do not be afraid to pick the person who is not the best player, because that will make you a better person and a stronger player. Choosing the hardest right, is often where you will experience the most growth.

The more you realize and accept your talents as true gifts from God, the more comfortable you will feel using your gifts. The more comfortable you become, the more you will start to truly see how your unique talents and gifts can bless other people. When you acknowledge the blessings that others have received because of you, the more you will want to share. And in those sharing moments you will begin to see your very own rewards from you functioning at your highest potential.

Do everything with a purpose and be great at all that you do. Unapologetically, share your gifts and talents so this world is given meaning because of you! I love you more than you know, and I am your biggest cheerleader, and loudest voice you hear from the sidelines.

Love Always...Mom

A Note to My Black Son Darian, My DJ…

From the moment your father and I heard the echo of your heartbeat at our first ultrasound, our lives were forever changed. I immediately fell in love with the dream of you. You see, I had lived a pretty full life being aunt and godparent to so many. Finally, a child of my own with the Man that I love!

I want you to know that life can be beautiful, fulfilling, and everything that you could ever want and more. When I look into your eyes, I get a glimpse into the chambers of your heart. A heart that is filled with the joys of a young child. Like learning to ride a bike, playing video games with your friends, or shooting hoops with your Dad. But I also see how much it hurts when you fall off that bike and skin your knee, or when I see you hang your head when your friends find new friends. And after hours of playing basketball with your Dad, being tutored and nurtured, only to try out for the team and not be chosen. I feel that pain, that disappointment, and hurt. I realize that as much as I try, nothing I do will prevent your heart from being broken. I have to hold back the tears when I think of the many times that you will face disappointment, when others you care about let you down or when you are faced with the cruelty of this world and feel alone.

I love you so much, DJ. I wish that I could hold your hand and walk you through each phase of your life, but I know the day will come when I and your father will have to let your hand go and will have to watch as you walk away from us and into a world that we worked so hard to prepare you for. Remember that you are loved, that you are special, that you are strong, that you are important, that you are beloved. And that as much as I love you, your Father in Heaven loves you more. He can heal your heart, and give you the courage to love again. Give Jesus all of your disappointments, all of your fears and He will replace them with the courage to defeat the many challenges of life.

I love you so much DJ.

Love Always…Mommy

A Note to My Black Son Julian, My Poopie Doo…

To say that you mean the world to me would be an understatement for sure! To say that I can even remember what my life was like before you arrived would be untruthful. To say that you choosing me to be your Mommy made me the luckiest girl in the world would be the truest words ever spoken!

As I have told you before, when I found out at the young age of twenty-one that I would soon become somebody's Mother, I was unbelievably terrified!!! Do you hear me?!? Lol I just knew I would be an epic failure. However, ten years later, my life has transformed in unimaginable ways!

I once believed that I brought you into the world to only love and mold you when this is truly an even exchange. We learn and we grow together. Being your Mother has been the most frighteningly beautiful experience. I cherish our level of communication; it is rare and I pray you continue to feel comfortable enough to share all of your dreams, nightmares, heartbreaks, and desires with me! You possess such a cool and confident demeanor in everything you put your mind to. You never hesitate to tell me when I am your inspiration. You inspire me as well!!

Seeing an extension of me grow and observing certain traits mimic those of my own is a sight to see! When you find me staring, just know I am only awe of what God has allowed me to create and experience!

Our Mommy and Son bond will be adored eternally! I pray that I am doing my job well enough that it shapes you into a productive and compassionate member of society. My ultimate prayer is that you and the family you create continue our legacy of love, laughter, and communication! I love you so much Julian Elijah! XOXOXO

Love Always…Mommy

Photo By: Sherri B. Photography

A Note to My Black Son William H Robinson IV aka Liam......

At the time I am writing this, you are only 7 years old. You have yet to experience life as a Black Man. Lucky for you right now, you are oblivious to the dangers this world has for you. You are the comic relief to the family, and you speak words of wisdom that are far beyond your years. You still possess a sense of innocence that allows you to move freely through rooms and be your authentic self without fear of judgement.

You have had an almost perfect life except for the passing of your father. I never wanted you to be another statistic of a Black Man without a father. I married him before you were born to ensure that you had a two-parent home. He too was a Black Man, who was so burdened that God saw fit to take him home. You have so much of him in you, which is not always a good thing LOL. Despite your father's flaws, one thing I can say for certain is he loved you. The day he found out you were a boy he knew you were definitely carrying on the family name. Thus making you the fourth. You have the name of a King and I want you to know do not ever let anyone remove your crown.

As a woMan I will never know what it is like to be a Black Man. I often ask myself how can I raise one? How do I explain to you that although you will always be my little boy, at some point the world will see you as a threat? How do I explain that the story of Emmitt Till still resonates today? How do I explain that I am scared that you will grow up to be successful and die in vain due to "fitting a description"? Right now, I do not have an answer. What I do know however, is that I do pray for you. I will never allow you to use your skin tone as an excuse not to be great. You are lineage is filled with too Many amazing Black men who refused to be a victim.

I once watched an interview with actor Mahershala Ali in which he stated that the difference between white men and Black Men is how they move through the world. He explained white male privilege is moving through the world playing offense. Black Men, however, have to always play defense. Meaning if you want to do something you already know there will be obstacles and you have to create a plan to overcome them. Until the system changes son, I want you to play the best defense in this world.

I promise to equip you with the tools of life so that no one will ever be able to tell you that you cannot do something. I will teach you about credit and finances. I will teach you about protection. I will teach you how to express yourself. Most importantly I will teach you that you can come to me no matter what and I will always be there.

Love Always...Mommy

A Note to My Black Son Big Jet...

I wanted to thank you for helping me grow, mature and slow down. Thank you for helping me appreciate every single day. Thank you for teaching me to think before I react. And thank God for choosing me to be your mommy.

Why do I call you Big Jet? Because even at your current age of 5, I know you have a Big future. You fill the room with your presence, and I am constantly impressed with your creativity already at such a young age. As much as I would like for you to stay little forever, I cannot wait to see all the amazing things you are going to do. I pray this world never changes you. They may not see you the way I do but that is ok because you will always have me! You are growing up so fast, but I guess that is what happens when you are named Jet.

Love Always...Mommy

A Note to My Black Son Angelo…

Dear Pooh Man, my Son who I love….

Strength
Poise
Confidence
Empathy
Integrity
Compassion
Respect

Angelo, my Son who I love, you already exhibit the strength to lead and the faith to follow.
Angelo, my Son who I love, you already walk and carry yourself with the poise of a King!
Angelo, my Son who I love, you already walk with the confidence of a lion!
Angelo, my Son who I love, you have an empathic heart and caring nature that makes me proud to be your Mother.
Angelo, my Son who I love, you already conduct yourself with integrity and strive to do what is right-which are qualities that are valued in not only a Man, but also a person.
Angelo, my Son who I love, you show the compassion of Christ in your heart.
Angelo, my Son who I love, you must demand the respect and honor you require from everyone you encounter!

Angelo my Son, I love you more than you will ever know!

Love Always…Mommy

A Note to My Black Son Bradford…

Words cannot begin to describe how incredibly grateful I am that God chose me to be YOUR mother. You are a kind and compassionate soul. Your work ethic is unmatched. You are definitely a formidable opponent when it comes to anything academic. Your work ethic makes me so proud and inspires me to be better. Your tenacity to persevere and get difficult tasks accomplished is amazing to me. I am in awe of the way you balance humility and brilliance. Our Heavenly Father has been gracious to you and has favored you and I am thankful.

I am so excited as you begin this next chapter of your life, endeavoring to tell stories in your own unique way. I believe God has so much in store for you and will use you to touch many people in incredible ways through the gifts he has placed in you.

*My son be strong and courageous! My eternal prayer for you is that you walk confidently in the gifts that God has blessed you with. I pray **Colossians 1:9-12 (NKJV)** over you always, which says, "…I do not cease to pray for you, and to ask that you may be filled with the knowledge of His will in all wisdom and spiritual understanding; that you may walk worthy of the Lord, fully pleasing Him, being fruitful in every good work and increasing in the knowledge of God; strengthened with all might, according to His glorious power." I believe in you and I know you will do great things and tell impactful stories.*

Thank you for the joy you bring to our family and for doing life with us. Being your mom has been AND IS the greatest blessing of my life.

Love Always…Mom

Photo By: Kamron Khan Photography

A Note to My Black Son Myles T., My Pooder, My Stinka-Man My Meatball…

Words cannot express the love I felt when I saw your little face on that beautiful Wednesday September 1st morning. You changed my life that day for the best. Who knew someone so small could make me feel so whole?

I have great plans for you, but I want you to have great plans for yourself. I believe in you no matter what choices you make in life. Do what is best for you and be a good leader.

The world can and will be tough at times, but as long as you keep God in your vision and heart, nothing will defeat you. I love you more than any words or gifts can express.

Be you, but always be mindful of other's feelings. You are such a handsome, young man. You are truly blessed; never forget it.

May I be blessed to see you become the man God and I want you to be.

Remember this:

> *Have I not commanded you? Be strong and courageous. Do not be frightened, and do not be dismayed, for the Lord your God is with you wherever you go.* ***(Joshua 1:9 KJV)***

Love Always…Mommy

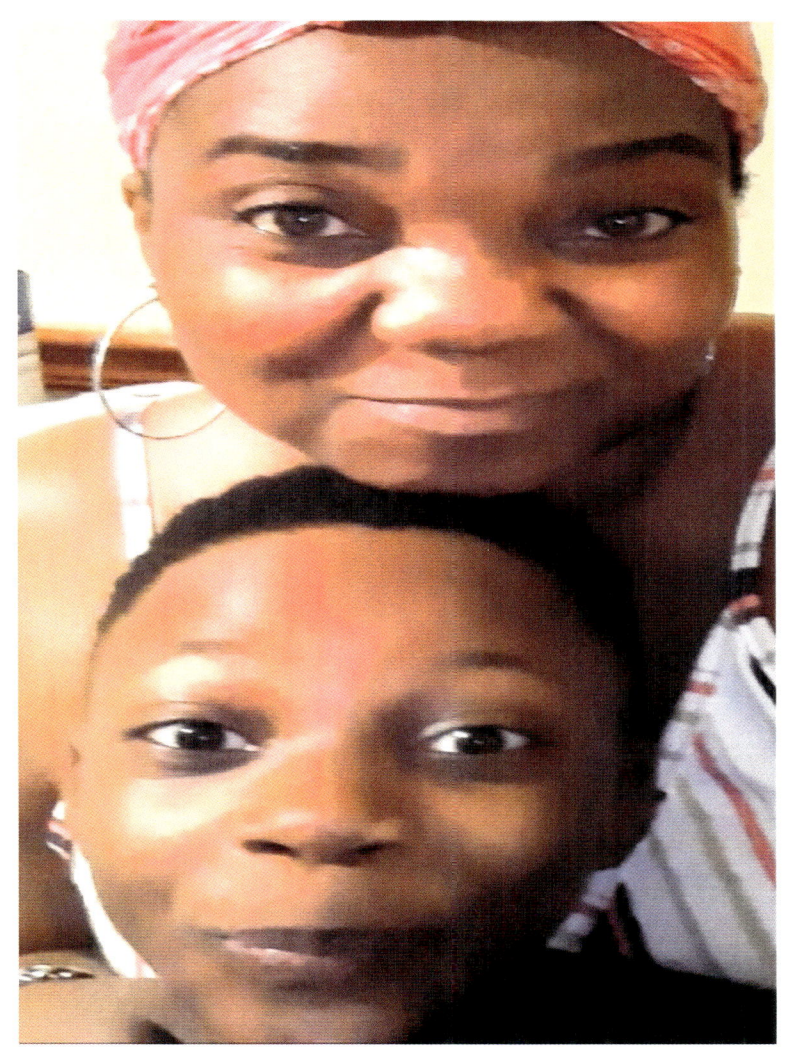

A Note to My Black Son KB...

Only life experience will show you how powerful you truly are. When I first laid my eyes on you, I knew you were special. Your spirit was different. You are growing up in a time that does not celebrate you based solely on the color of your skin. Do not be distracted by the noise, do not fear growing into your purpose. You were built for a time such as this. You are God's masterpiece, own it and thrive in it.

I know you will do something of impact when you transition into manhood. But I want you to remember these few things forever. God loves you no matter what, you are never alone as long as you abide in Him. As your Papa always said, "Keep God first as the head of your life." Equip yourself with all the wisdom my Dad poured into you when you were so young. Second, being authentically you is and will always be the cool thing to do. You will know you are being authentic because your heart, mind, and soul will agree. Trust your process; life is all about finding your way, embracing your journey and walking in your true purpose. It will not always look like what you want it to but know you are resilient, and you must stay planted to see your vision through. Respect your sphere of influence and know sometimes the lesson is not about you but those who are attached to you. We are all given assignments, never take it lightly or for granted. Lead with love. Real men do cry, real men do feel, real men do provide. How you show love is an outward reflection of your love for God. God is love.

When life beats you down, remember who you are and who you belong to. You are not ordinary or basic, the calling on your life is bigger than you know at the moment. I will always love you unconditionally and wholeheartedly, never forget that Future King.

Love Always...Mommy

Black Mon & Toddler Illustration By: Rodney Potts

A Note to My Black Son Robert, affectionately known as Bobby…

For as long as I can remember, I always wanted to be a Mother, but more importantly, I wanted to be a Mother to a "SON". A word that has more meaning than the three letters used to spell it. A Son who will carry the family's last name for as-long-as he shall live; a Son who stands in the stead of his Father, whether he is absent or present. A Son, although born a male child, has the heart of his mother. A son who looks for and wants his Son's approval. Whatever transpires throughout their lifetime, he will always be "my Son!"

Well, God gave me you! A chocolate, curly head, 8 lb.8 oz. bouncing, baby Boy. A blessing to those who take the time to know you and those you briefly exchange a few kind words or even just a nod. Whatever the exchange, I will say this, continue to move forward utilizing the gifts that you were given as a child, and now a man, a Black Man, who knows no boundaries, who knows that through Christ, "All Things Are Possible!" Remember, you were created with purpose, and there is so much more in you. Stand tall so you can reach the unreachable, and draw from all your resources, so you may obtain the unattainable. Greatness resides within you, it gives substance and meaning to your hopes and dreams you spent countless hours explaining to me on how they could work. 'Laughing out loud'

Nevertheless, we are living in times of uncertainty. Nothing is or is like what it used to be. So never be afraid to begin again. Step boldly into what you believe and what you want from life. You only get out, what you put in. Know that I am one of your biggest fans, and supporters, I am here for you, cheering for you, loving you and encouraging you. You are my Black Son in whom I am well pleased.

Love Always…Your Ma

A Note to My Black Son Ethan, My Boogie Baby, My Prince…

Today is the day before your 3ʳᵈ birthday and you are starting pre-school in a few days. I have seen strength in you that I did not know could exist within a toddler. You are fierce, you have a fire in your soul, a passion in your personality, you are intelligent, a genius (your word for you), you are a future King! As you weave your way through life keep your fire and do not let ANYONE put it out, not even me! The strength you have been given is directly from God, he took two of his strongest people to create a Man who would be a Lion and a Dragon! Let your voice roar mighty like the Lion do not ever be afraid! God has given you a reason and a purpose, your life is meant to be. On your darkest day, at your darkest hour, remember darkness is the place where life is created it is the beginning of all things. You send your prayers to God in the dark and they manifest in the light, you place a seed in the ground it grows in the dark and reaches for the light, you were created in the dark in my womb for 10 months, then you were born into the light. DO NOT BE SCARED OF THE DARK you must go through the dark to get to the light. If it ever gets too dark, God gave you a voice of fire and like the fierce and mystical Dragon you are to use your God given voice to light the way. I will be with you throughout your journey physically and/or spiritually. Life is a journey, an amalgamation of experiences used to create the best you, you are not just Ethan you are a soul. It is your job to learn, grow, and eventually transcend!

As I close this letter remember these seven jewels my Son: 1. Listen to your heart, trust your instincts, and ask yourself does this sit well with my soul? (This question is for you and only you!) 2. Love the Dark-darkness is the beginning of the creation of all 3. Know thyself-learn who you are, learn where you come from; learn who is inside you (that is key). You are a soul my son, look past humanity, think deeper, it is your soul that is who you are. 4. Man is to have a wife-you were not put here to be alone. Find her, love her, cherish her, respect her, and carry on our family with her! 5. Respect yourself and others-give respect to everyone to get it for yourself. If someone does not give it demand it, if they still do not give it, fall back, let Karma be their teacher. 6. The Black Woman is a Queen-she will be here for you, she will love you, she will create the type of family you come from and need for the continuation of your legacy. Protect her, provide for her, place her above all else and she will do the same for you. 7. The Black Man is King-Learn like a King, behave like a King, interact with other Kings, lead another Black Man to his true self as King, raise your Sons to be Kings!

I love you with everything in my soul and souls are eternal. Our love is forever young Prince, future King!

Love Always…Mommy

A Note to My Black Son My Darling DeMar…

You are everything a mom could ever wish for in a son. Your work ethic and your mannerisms are impeccable. You are truly a man's man. Life was not a rose garden but your pulled out all the thorns and succeeded in life; for this, I salute you. When men in this day fall short, you stand quite tall. I admire the way you cover your family. Sometimes when I am in your presence, I stare at the man you have grown into. You are an inspiration and role model to many other males. The way you often take the low road or you are called upon for your knowledge and wisdom makes my heart swell and to think, you are my first born. I will love you forever and a day!

Love Always…Mom

A Note to My Black Son My J.C.…

You are my teddy bear of a son with the biggest heart in the world. You are so giving and that trait can scare a mother; you always think of others first and yourself last. I would like to see you focus a lot more on your future. You are a bright star with lots of potential. Reach for the sky my love because you have all you need to get there…Just do it! I will love you forever and a day!

Love Always…Momma

A Note to My Black Son My Darling Reese Pooh…

A handsome devil you are; what one would say a "lady's man". Just saying your name brings a smile to my face (at times). You are the most spoiled of your siblings but trust in you, one can do. I listen to you while you converse with others and you give people honesty. You are a man on solid ground. I need to say, in life, you are going to have to have a little more patience and understanding for others; forgiveness is the key to life. You are often judged by your past but do not let your past define who you are; rise, yes RISE above it because it is never too late to get it right! I will love you forever and a day!

Love Always…Mom

A Note to My Black Sons Stephen and Joshua…

Names are significant in many cultures for example amongst the Igbos and Yorubas. Both of your names are significant and meaningful. Apart from your Igbo and Yoruba names that are indicative of my and your father's culture, your first names also reflect our family values:

❖ *Stephen is derived from Greek which means crown. You are royalty and set apart for great things and honor. Remember that!*

❖ *Joshua, your name is Jewish and it means Jehovah saves or savior. We have God as our salvation, strength and anchor. Remember that!*

*My dear sons, the greatest thing you must remember is love. In **1 Corinthians 13:1-13**, we learn that love is powerful and Love is above all things. That is because God is love. If you love God, you will live right, act right, do right, and be right. So, Remember that!*

Love Always…Mom

A Note to My Black Son (Monster, Handsome, Boy) Max...

I praise God for you, your sister and your brother; you all have taught me to love life more deeply with your dad. I am proud of how you evolved. Before you turned three, you realized that you did not like being an only child. You asked if dad and I would be able to give you siblings. God blessed you with two and you did not disappoint as a big brother! You have shown how grateful you were to have both a little sister and brother; we appreciate you.

I will never forget when you came home from Kindergarten to share that you learned about the life and death of Dr. Martin Luther King, Jr. You cried that day like it was the day he died. Dad and I explained how serious, sick and sad it is in America-unarmed Black Men are hunted. Recently, we have discussed that Black Men are criminalized, killed and frequently it is by law enforcement. I truly regret that both your dad's older brother and my older sister died before you were born. You made me really sad when you told me that you expect to die young because your late uncle was killed and aunt died ill; I balled and did not sleep that night.

*Pray, play every day, study the Bible, rest on the Sabbath and be at peace; enjoy silence. Your innocence and the truth are not enough to protect you; trust no one (see: **Psalms 118:8-9** & **Jeremiah 17:7**). Have faith seeing, "...we know that all things work together for good to them that love God, to them who are the called according to his purpose." **(Romans 8:28 KJV)** It is hard to ensure safety, find beauty and share gratitude in the world. Be kind, patient, pursue the arts, athletics and academics. Your purpose is to excel; you are young, gifted and Black.*

Love Always...Momma

A Note to My Black Son (Boy Boy, Cute, Mr.) Clint,

I grew up with two big sisters but I had no brothers at home. Being a mom of three is an adventure. Especially since you are curious, interactive and want to learn. With this in mind we did our best to help you learn as much as you could before pre-school/Kinder. I was excited when you were able to join your brother and sister in elementary school. I saw how sad you got after the COVID-19 pandemic closed school. I am your proctor until you can return to school safely; we will do ELA, Math and the EVSA STEM Specials together at home.

*Thanks for the prayers and continue to praise God as in **Psalms 146**. It is okay that Mom is not working now; I love being a sister, daughter, aunt, wife and Mom! Be polite, prepared, patient and persistent in the First Grade. You will have a firm foundation when you leave home to do good work in the world. Be blessed as Christ taught in **Matthew 5:3-17**. At five years old, you have an office (desk, chair and PC), I thank God you see yourself as a boss!*

Love Always...Mom

A Note to My Black Son Brendan, My Baby Boy, My Big Boy, My Sweet Pea, My Baby Bear, My Petey Pie, My Love Bug, My Doodlebug, My Doobie, My Doo. And now, My Man Child…

From the moment I knew I was carrying you, immediately I only wanted the absolute best for you. I knew I wanted to be the best Mom ever, wanting to be able to give you all that you needed, and most of the things you wanted. And once I found out I was carrying my young prince? I wanted it ALL for you!! The possibilities were infinite. I knew we would spend endless hours on a field, diamond, court, or in a gym, and I could not wait. I was ready to be that sports Mom. T-Ball, baseball, football, wrestling, swimming, track & field…. But education was absolutely and without question first and foremost.

Brilliant in your own right, school has never been your favorite. However, with any and everything you do, it has all rested on a decision. No different when it came to education. When it had to be done, you put your mind to it, and did it; you just had to put in the work. It was there all along; something I told you over and over and over again, but you had to learn this for yourself. School brought lessons beyond the books. Life lessons-priorities, friendships, truths and some painful realities.

Watching you do well in most everything you did, and then excel in football and baseball gave me great pride. You gave and continue to give your all when you are out there. Your passion for your sport, your craft is a joy to watch; it is an experience. From your preparation, to your entrance on the field; from the starting whistle of the game to the final buzz of the clock, you leave it all on the field. You have just taken part in the B95N Experience.

We cannot speak of all you are and will be, without addressing what is. Our nation is in racial turmoil, and you and all of our Brown Boys (and Men) are a target and in danger. "They" are fearful of the greatness you possess and want to rid the world of you, but you and all you possess are here to stay. You are fearfully and wonderfully made, a Son of The King, an Heir to the Throne, a Child of the Most High. Although in my humanness, every time you walk out the door, I fear you will not return. But you have been prayed for and prayed over, by those here, and those that came before you who are long gone. We know you are covered and protected by our Lord and Savior.

You have been the absolute apple of my eye, and wind beneath my wings. I have so enjoyed being your Mother, and I know in spite of the current climate of the nation, our best is yet to come. My one and only, my Prince, continue to blaze your path of greatness and walk into your destiny. Leave your mark and your legacy, so the world never forgets who you are/were.

Love Always…Mommi

A Note to My Black Son Lamar Jr., My Little Man…

The year is 2020. A lot has happened this year since you were born: violence, protesting, and a world pandemic called the Coronavirus (AKA COVID19). In January, one of the greatest basketball players of all time, Kobe Bryant, died in a horrific helicopter crash along with his daughter and 7 others. In March, a pandemic occurred in various parts of the world first before hitting America where hundreds of thousands of people died. In the middle of the pandemic, an innocent Black Man, George Floyd, was killed by the hands of police in Minneapolis, MN. Unfortunately, this is an all too familiar occurrence in America where Black Men and Black Women are killed by crooked cops or other racist people.

Son, I pray that you will be judged by your character, how you carry yourself and treat people, NOT by the color of your skin. Being a Black Boy/ Man in America is hard because of the hate in some people's hearts. These people focus too much on color, the one thing we cannot change, rather than character. I am so sorry that this occurs and I pray every day that it will not be this way much longer. The truth is, there will always be hateful people in the world. I also pray that you will never experience the hate that Tamir Rice, Trayvon Martin, George Floyd, and so many others experienced.

Son, I want you to live a good life, strive to be the best version of you, and treat everyone with respect, the same way you want to be treated (the Golden Rule). There will be some who will not like you. Do not worry about them. Do not hate the haters; rather use them as motivators to do what is right and what is you. Think for yourself, do not follow the crowd. Love God, family, friends and treat people with respect regardless of how they treat you. I pray that you will grow up to be a mighty man of valor in God's eyes. God created you with purpose in mind; it is your job to fulfill that purpose. You are to add to the world, not take from it. You are above, not beneath. You are handsome. You are special. You are loved. You are gifted and you are intelligent. Use these gifts and abilities to bring glory to God by serving and helping others. You are a Black Boy, who will eventually become a Black Man, living in America.

Love always…Mommy

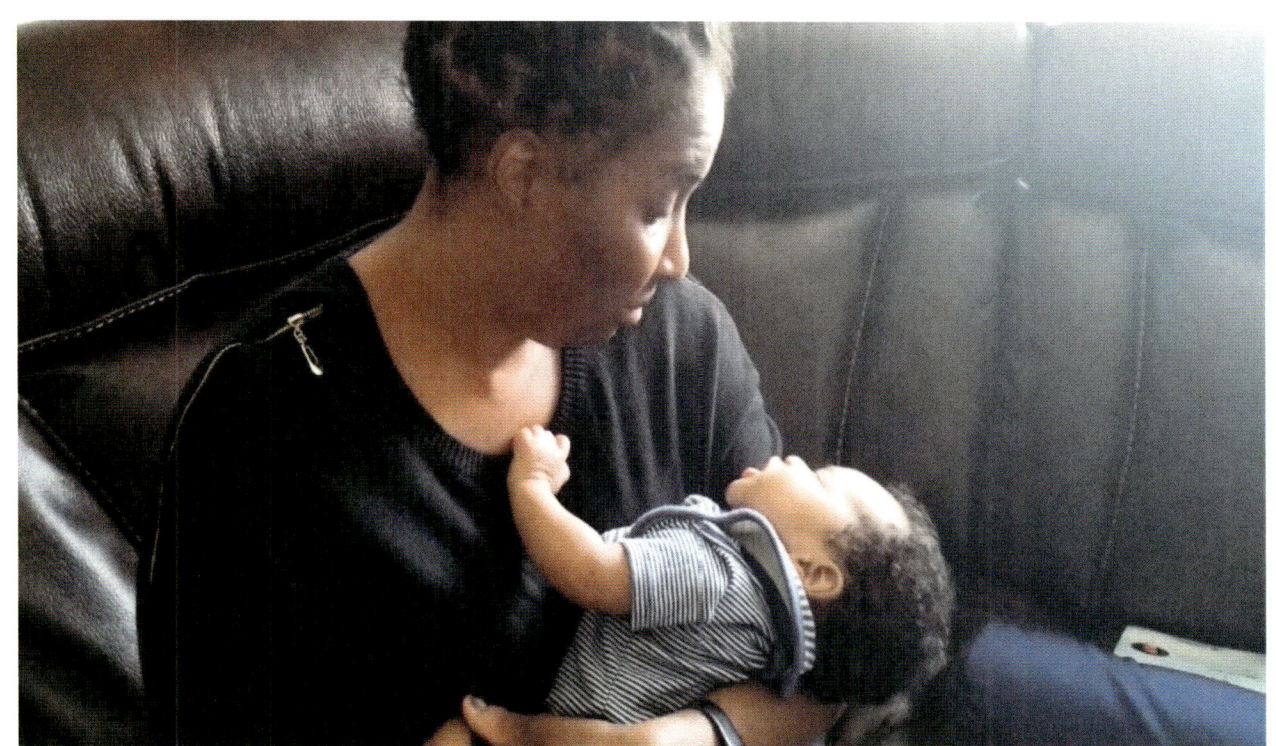

A Note to My Black Son Tony…

You are pure light. Not just spiritually, but physically. The melanin in your skin that makes your skin dark is ironically, scientifically, living light. In moments when you do not feel like pure light, it is not because you are not, it is because you have forgotten what (not who) you are.

The world, man's world, can do that to you, but only if you let it.

In this lifetime, in this life form, you are a spiritual being having a human experience. At times in your life, it will be easier to show up as one or the other, when in fact the lesson of this place we call Earth is to be both.

Your ancestors' life force runs through your physical and spiritual veins. Carrying lifetimes and light years of wisdom and growth. They charge you to stand tall and BE. In BEING, you represent their glory. You are evolution and elevation.

They call us Kings and Queens to remind us of our brilliance. Son, that represents only a fraction of who (not what) you are.

You are a light being in a beautiful Earth tone body. You are capable of every day miracles in just… being…you. Living light flows from your fingertips. Create with it, build with it, play and have fun with it. There will even be times when you need to deconstruct with it. No matter the case BE IT. You do not have to DO anything to be living light. You simply have to REMEMBER WHAT YOU ARE!

A few things I learned along the way that may help you:

- *Laugh and have fun every day; joy is a choice that begins with gratitude.*
- *Relationships matter; with universal life force, family, friends and even those with whom you disagree.*
- *Be more motivated by joy than pain; the process of growth can be done with joy.*
- *You are worthy – period, so honor yourself in all things; the only moments in life that I had regret for at one time or another, all had one thing in common, I did not value myself at the time of the decision.*
- *Let go of any programming I gave you that does not serve you. I did not know any better.*

Finally, thank you for choosing me as your parent. There is nowhere, on this plane or the next, that my unconditional love for you cannot reach you. I love you more…

Love Always…Mom

A Note to My Black Sons Ian and Eli…

I have always been so proud of the adversity that you have overcome living in two worlds with almost completely different cultures on each side of our family. You have endured poverty, the politics of living in a middle class socio-economical background as a minority, as well as overt and covert racism from your Caucasian and African American family members, and you have done this all with a good attitude, fortitude and sense of strength that it not normally seen in children so young.

I want you both to reach for the stars and know in your heart that you can do ANYTHING that you set your mind to. I want you to know that your African American side of the family loves you unconditionally and supports you 100% in all of your endeavors. We are here to listen to you and empathize with you. I do not want you to hold back any of your feelings whether it is anguish, joy, confusion or indifference. I want you to feel free to talk about everything that is on your mind without fear of belittling and judgement. The world we live in is a tough place right now and I want you to feel that being with your Momma is comforting and with boundless love.

I love you so much, Ian and Eli. Go and change the world like the Kings you are and are meant to be.

Love always…Momma

A Note to My Black Sons Cole & Brad...

*As I look at you both, I am reminded of how blessed I am to have the honor of being your Mother. To be able to see you grow from precarious little babies to strategic, goal oriented young Men is astonishing. There is so much I love about you- from your athletic abilities, academic successes and loving personalities, to your behavioral and social graces but the most important thing I love about you is your love for the Lord. While beauty, charm and wit are all entertaining they are also all fleeting and what you two encompass with your love for the Lord lasts for eternity and equips all your positive characteristics to thrive. Although you are both young Men and have different levels of life to experience, the fact you are grasping on to a beautiful moral compass at such a young age will truly benefit you as you age. While it is easy as your Mother, to enable you and not acknowledge/address properly your flaws, areas of weakness or wrongdoings, I have the task of creating and supporting Men that will be part of the elite group that are faithful, committed, honest, balanced, confident (not cocky), humble, even tempered, courageous, respectful, intelligent, responsible, loving, hardworking, emotionally and spiritually mature. By doing that, I too must submit to acknowledging my flaws as well so I can properly guide you. My goal is that our Mother/Son partnership is not superficial, does not just stroke your egos or mine but stems deep where we reveal and confess our flaws, shortcomings and mistakes so that we may earnestly grow from away from them; becoming people who do more good than harm to ourselves and those around us. Because my Sons, "If a tree has strong roots, not even the strongest of hands can pluck it from where it stands."-M. Dhilwayo. In this world, where we face unprecedented people and times, I certainly have many fears for you as Black Men because unfortunately, those part of the blind world do not see/know and/or respect the types of young Men you are internally, the strong legacies that have been laid out before you, sowed into you and what all you have already positively contributed to society. These broken people just see what supports their own insecurities and fears and all you can continue to do is trust in the Lord to be your protector and then do YOUR parts by continuing to stand tall and bold as Men filled with knowledge, wisdom, power and integrity. I have no doubt in my mind that you two, as it is written in **1 Timothy 4:12 (NIV)** "will be an example to the believers in word, in conduct, in love, in spirit, in faith, in purity." You are on the right paths my mighty Sons and have a village behind you that is praying, pushing for your successes to continue and blossom into fruition. I am so proud of you; words cannot express the love I have for you. While you charter into seen and unseen territories always keep in mind the words of your dear Grandparents "Always remember to love God completely, love yourselves correctly and love others compassionately "and I promise you the world will see and feel the impact of who you both are and will become.*

Love Always...Ma-ma

A Note to My Black Son Jalon…

Named after your Dad and both Grand Fathers. Men of emotional, mental, and physical strength. Men that exude family and the well-being of others. Men of God. Jalon, you are an extension of unconditional love and kindness. We prayed for your health, happiness, and that you would know love. You are beyond our most imaginative dreams. We have been blessed to watch you grow and look forward to the awesome future that awaits the adult you.

Since the moment we learned we were pregnant with you, you have been an absolute enhancement to our lives. You are my love. I think the world of you. Your thunderous voice starts and ends my day. The corny jokes you tell followed by your own laughter makes me bend over in tears. The embellished conversations around the fire pit are captivating. I love your artwork-how you detail you and your Dad's locs. I love watching the serious engineering design efforts you and your sister (your biggest cheerleader) use while building forts out of couch cushions. My hands down moment of solitude comes from hearing you humming through the vents while you are independently playing in your room.

You are living proof just how much God loves me. You are my irreplaceable and precious gift, wrapped in everything good. Your existence motivates me daily to continue works for a better tomorrow, for you. Your hugs arm me with the support needed to travel throughout the day.

If no one ever tells you, please know: you are one strong, warm hearted, incredibly smart, uniquely aware, diversely talented, fun loving, gifted asset. Remember to always listen the first time. Do not give anyone power of you. Remember the men and women you come from and continue to build the legacy of self, family, and community. I am nothing but proud to be your Mom, today, tomorrow, and eternally.

You and me together.　　*Or even a train.*

On a boat.　　*I love you.*

Or even a goat.　　*And you love me.*

You and me forever.　　*You and me together.*

On a plane.　　*Kiss on the Bips.*

Love Always…Mommy

A Note to My Black Son Michael A.K.A. Mikey…

Before you were born, I always wondered how you would be. I wondered how you would act, who you would mostly favor, and whose mannerisms you would have; so excited to meet my baby Boy. When I saw you for the first time, it was love at first sight! Such a perfect creation and so thankful to be blessed with such a gift as you.

As I have watched you grow and develop into your own, I could not be prouder. You are intelligent, kind-hearted, caring and so handsome! All the things a Mother could ask for. I pray that you utilize all that I have taught you and instilled in you thus far. I also want to prepare you for a world that may not embrace you like I do. This world may not treat or understand your good-natured spirit or your open heart. They may not return the love and respect you give others. Do not let that change who you are. Do not conform to the way the world wants you to be. Stand apart and firm on what you know to be right and true.

This world we live in is ever changing. So many cruel and evil spirits around to distract you and detour you from your path. Keep God first and always with you, for He will never forsake you. Be a leader in all you do and try to make choices that best work in your favor according to the Lord's teachings and He will guide you all the way.

You never realize how much you want to say until someone asks you to do so. I have never taken the time to write a letter expressing things I would like to say to you and for you to keep with you. I pray that you keep me in your heart always and when you become afraid, lost, or lonely, think of Mommy and I will be with you. I am so thankful for this keep sake memoir of a special note just for you. I hope you enjoy reading this as much as I enjoyed writing it and I promise this will not be the last.

Love Always…Mommy

A Note to My Black Son KJ…

I am writing this letter to let you know how much I love you. It is not that I am concerned or doubt you know this, but rather my words will ring in your heart forever. Let us be honest, those words will ring in your ears right when you need it the most. The reality of it all is life is not always kind to us. People do not necessarily treat us the way we deserve to be treated. It is in those times that you need to know someone cares, and they are right here for you. That someone is ME!

*I can remember the day the doctor informed your Dad and I that we were having a boy. I do not know who cried more, me or your Dad. We were extremely excited especially after having 3 beautiful daughters. During delivery there were complications and I recalled praying and petitioning the Lord about you. I spoke the word over your unborn life and declared life. **Psalms 118:17** He honored my request.*

Now 19 years later you are here, handsome, witty, strong and full of potential. I often reference you as my "one and only". That is truly who you are to me: my future engineer. I wish our celebration could continue this way but unfortunately life could take a turn and you could find yourself having to deal with things in your life that you would rather not face.

Do not fret: keep your head up. If you fall get back up and try it again. As those curveballs fly your way, just know I am a call away. You have already experienced tough times, I know that. Challenges during high school when the thought of going to class each day increased your stress level. It is extremely unfortunate that the system failed you. On behalf of all those that let you down, "I Apologize". Despite the pain you suffered, you need to know that those tough times cannot define you. Look at them as experiences that came to make you stronger.

*Looking at you now makes me extremely proud because you persevered through it all. You made it, and you will do it again, and again. God showed up on your behalf, took you by the hand and lead you through every trial, every tribulation. He has truly been a cornerstone for us. Go forth Son and be the best Black Man that you can be. Let nothing dull your shine and no one define your destiny. Keep your head up and stay in the game. And above all keep God first. Let **Matthew 6:22** guide you and define your territory. You can and you will make it! Kevin L. Smith Jr., my engineer will do great things; I believe that with my whole heart and I cannot wait to see you soar.*

Love Always…Mom

A Note to My Black Sons Randall and Robby, My Whys, My Forever Loves…

Before I met the two of you, I loved you beyond limits. I created an image of who you would be before ever setting eyes on your beautiful faces. I tried to predict who you would be as individuals, your personalities, your dreams and your desires. What became abundantly clear was that my desires for you paled in comparison to the reality of what the two of you have become.

You amaze me and keep me often in awe and exceed my expectations of you every day. The memories that we create will remain forever etched in my heart. Even when you are grown Men and depart from me, know that I am with you forever and always.

*I never thought that I could love in this capacity; sometimes the love I have for the two of you cannot be put into words. I hope that I have created a foundation for you that will allow for your continued growth so that you may achieve all of your goals and dreams. Know that I will always be your biggest fan, your cheerleader and will **always** be there to catch you when you fall. For your first heartbreak, your first disappointment, or your first epic fail, know that you will have a soft place to land, an awaiting embrace and understanding without judgement from me.*

I have made you both promise me to always stay my babies and I will always hold you to that promise. No matter how tall and big the two of you may get, I will always see you as my babies and there is nothing you can do to change that.

It is my hope that I have painted the stage for what the love of a woman should feel like so that when you search for your forever partner, you will find that special someone who is worthy of your heart. I am so proud of the two of you. I know you were placed in my life and on this Earth to do something great. I am ready to witness your greatness and see the final manifestations of the greatness that the two of you possess. I love you to the moon and beyond.

Love Always…Mommy

A Note to My Black Son B.J….

Being a Mother does not come with a handbook; it is all about trial and error. I worry a lot because I want to make sure that I protect you at all costs. I want to protect you from this sick world we live in.

I love you, Son. You changed my life for the better and I want to do my very best by giving you everything you deserve and more. You were born during a worldwide shutdown. During this shutdown, there have been riots, looting and killings done by police officers who really had no reason to pull their triggers. Almost all of the people killed were Black Men simply because they were BLACK. I am not telling you this to scare you but I want you to know that I will do my best in preparing you for this world that is not fair to Black people but especially to Black Men. I will do my best to raise you to be the best BLACK MAN you can be in a not so free world. I love you, son!

Love Always…Mom

A Note to My Black Son Shorts, My Twin, My Peanut Butter Baby…

You have always been a light and a leader. From the time you were born, I saw me in you. You are a loving, caring, gentle spirit. I am so very proud of the man that you have become. I look forward to your future and all that is coming to you. You are my first born and although I spent more time picking you up from police departments when you were younger I knew that you would get it together and come out on top, and you have. I love you to life Twin always know that!

Love Always…Dukes

A Note to My Black Son Keith, My Baby Boy, My Hershey's Chocolate Baby…

You have always been my creative, imaginative child (like ya' mama). You are my middle "Sun" and to watch you grow into a great man and an amazing father has just made my spirit happy. I know there have been some ups and downs in your life, but you came out a better man with a shit load of confidence. Sometimes, we must go through things to become who we are supposed to be, and you have. There is so much more in store for you Baby Boy and I cannot wait to see how it all unfolds. Know that I love you to life Baby Boy!

Love Always…Ma Dukes

A Note to My Black Grandsons: Jordan, My CodyJo, My Reese's Cup Baby & Little Keith, My BamBam, My Hershey's Kiss Baby…

Oh, how I love me some of you 2!! There is no joy like that of being your Big Mama!! You both have so much good juju (Of course you would, look at who ya Big Mama is; it is in your blood!) My CodyJo, you were my first grandson and you filled a place in my heart that I did not know was void. I pray that you keep your active, never give up attitude and loving spirit. It is going to take you to so many phenomenal places and when you get there, know that I will be there with you cheering you on and supporting you! And to My BamBam with your Beautiful Brown Skin; your smile just lights up my heart. You are a strong, powerful, loving spirit with a zeal for life. With your high vibration, I cannot wait to see the man you will become; Big Mama will be right there lifting you up and encouraging you!! I Love you both to life!!

Love Always…Big Mama

A Note to My Black Son Ean, My Duke….

Even before conception, I prayed for you. As we shared a body, I felt you would be the male child to make me a "Boy-Mom." Even before I laid eyes on you, hearing them call you "Ean", alerting our family that you were indeed my SON (the answer to my prayers) did something to my soul. To this day, I cannot explain it. Before we met, my life had taken turns that had me lost. I had forgotten my purpose, I was existing, but not living. Then God sent me you. I gave you life, but you, Ean Johann, saved mine.

When you were small, I kept you close. I knew you were safe. I vowed to go up against anyone who threatened that protection…anyone. Then you started growing up, so I did too. I began to realize that no matter the effort, I could not shield you from the evils and injustices of this world; that frightens me. The answer to my prayers also has the leading role in my nightmares. I cower at the thought of your caramel brown skin, hairstyle or fashion choices being viewed as a threat or worse, as a crime, yet your talent, worthiness, intelligence and gentle spirit may well be overlooked. Knowing that I cannot always be with you helping you make sense of society's view of the Black Man and what that means for you, terrifies me in ways I cannot articulate.

*Failing to perfectly help you navigate the boundary between walking proudly in your purpose, taking thoughtful risks, chasing your dreams, standing up for what is right, using a rich vocabulary to keep you from being silenced **and** not doing any of the aforementioned just so you can stay free and alive shakes me to my core. When you have lost a husband, the thought of losing a Son is unbearable to say the least. How does a Mother instill a confident, independent voice in her Black Male Child while simultaneously teaching him to "be okay" with being muted? It is my job to make you feel secure being the young man you are destined to be.*

Contrarily, it is also my duty to help you realize that not everyone will appreciate your greatness or want to hear your voice. Your opinion will not always be valued. You see Ean, as your Mom, I have many jobs. I am also obligated to show you that I value all the things about you that the world will often ignore. I will love you through everything the world puts you through. You are not in this alone, physically present or not, I will always be on the battlefield with you. I will fight… just so you do not have to, not because you cannot defend yourself, but because it is safer. Just as I gave you life on the 12th day of October, 2006, I would lay down my life for you, even if it only added a single second to your life. I hate that I am forced to prepare you for a world that will undoubtedly disappoint and drain you and make you question your very existence. Please know when you are feeling that way, you have a Mother that will always be there to hold you, pick you up, and remind you to always believe in yourself. I challenge you to ask a friend if they have ever saved a life. See how special you have been since birth……. when you saved mine?

Love Always…Ma Dukes

Photo By: Stan Petrovsky (PictureUS//PhotoMyrtleBeach//StanWeddings)

A Note to My Black Sons Asim "AJ Rose Jr. & De'Sean M. Rose, My SONshines...

I gave birth to you all ten months apart at the tender age of 19 and 20. They forgot to include the instruction manual both times, lol. Seriously, the manual was never really needed, you all have been a joy to raise and watch mature. I hope life has been amazing for you all, because it was love at first sight twice for me. You know I have never been the mushy and affectionate type, so this is going to be short and sweet just like me (smile). This journey has not been easy, yet well worth it. I want you both to know how much you all mean to me. I am immensely proud of both of you. You are STRONG BLACK MEN (Eagle Scouts) destined for more greatness!!!! As you continue to find your way in this thing called life and adulthood, remember to keep God first and FOE (Family Over Everything). Remember every day is a new opportunity to make it great!

"Because of the LORD's great love we are not consumed, for his compassions never fail. They are new EVERY morning; Great is your faithfulness." (Lamentations 3:22-23 NIV) Keep making us proud. I love you!!!!!!!!!!!

Love Always...MA

Photo By: Drico Lamar

A Note to My Black Son Khalil, Pa…

From the very first time I felt you inside of me, I knew you were a true gift from God. You were destined to become the kind, loving, intelligent, and God-fearing Man you are today. To say I was frightened when you were delivered at 28 weeks (7 months) is an understatement. You were the toughest 2lb.4oz. baby Boy I had ever seen. As a new mom, it broke my heart every time I had to leave you at the hospital. However, God answered every one of my prayers and you came home 56 days after your birth.

Khalil you made raising you easy!! You followed all the rules, you did your homework and you listened when I told you to complete a task. As an only child, your creativity was astounding to me. You always managed to create the most beautiful artwork out of the simplest materials found in the house. Your thirst for knowledge and conversation about any topic made you mature beyond your years.

Do you know what I love about you the most? Your ability to see the good in people. Khalil, your loyalty and friendship to others truly impacts lives on a daily basis. Do not ever let anyone steal that away from you. When your heart was broken, it literally tore me up inside; however, you were resilient! You came out on the top! You did not let that situation kill the core essence of your soul. This type of spirit is definitely needed in the world you face as a BLACK MAN!!

Love Always…Mama

A Note to My Black Son Eric, My Walker…

When I was pregnant with you, I knew you were a boy. I also knew you would be named after your father as he would not have had it any other way. What can I say, you are all grown up now and have moved out of state to Virginia. You are a man, a Black Man. I am proud of you and more proud of you as a Black Man. With that said, it also scares me to death, to know you live in Virginia and for some reason, I still feel the need to protect you even from afar. I never want to be that Mom, you know that Mom; Trayvon Martin's Mom, Tamir Rice's Mom, Eric Garner's Mom, Breonna Taylor's Mom, and most recently James Blake's Mom, and all those other Moms that are on the list. They are no different from me; they are Moms too.

I want you to know I cannot believe how fast 26 years have gone by. Now that you are gone, I have more time to think and reflect. That little boy in the back seat of the car that told me he was a dumb reader is now a math teacher with Master's degree. That same little boy who got cheated out of his Pokémon cards and threw his lunch away every day is now a difference maker. I always believed in you. I always knew you were special. I always knew you could do anything. I admit, I was scared for you along the way because life has a way of eating us up. It tried to with all the stuff along the way and those mid-2000 years, with all those transitions, you still pushed through. You and your sister are different. She is a reactor and you are a processer. You process through your pain, get up, gather yourself, and move forward. All I can say as your Mom is, it has been a privilege raising you. I am honored God assigned me as YOUR Mom and trusted me with you. The truth is, you helped raise me too. You helped me be a better Mom and person. You made me think outside the box, be more patient, laugh when I wanted to cry, and showed me it is always all worth it.

Eric, as I have completely released you to your destiny, please know the best is yet to come. You will become an accomplished teacher, future school administrator, and beloved Coach Walker. You will marry a beautiful young lady who will know how to cook, and you will become a father that leaves a legacy to his children's children. You will become a pillar in your community, and you will follow your father's footsteps impacting others in the body of Christ.

My son, I am continually praying for you and as long as you keep Christ first, He will withhold nothing from you. So Eric, go fly! This Momma eagle has dropped you out the nest knowing God has you and you are going to soar! I am always here for you. I love you!

Jeremiah 29:11 & Philippians 4:13

Love Always…Mom

A Note to My Black Son My Dearest Cam...

I remember the day the doctor confirmed my suspicion that I was growing another baby, and a few months later, that you were a Boy. I was excited and frightened at the same time. This was not a world that had been kind to Black people, but especially not to our Black Boys and Men. So, how would your Dad and I raise you to be a force stronger than hate? To hold faith greater than fear? And to overcome any possible obstacle? There truly was no plan other than to love you to and through whatever came your way.

Then, on November 6, 1992, I met you face to face. It was in that very moment, the trajectory of my life changed. In partnership with your Dad, I knew all that I needed to know to support you on your Earthly journey. The answer was simply do all things through the lens of love adding filters of pure bliss, happiness and joy. This meant teaching you to love all regardless of differences; celebrate and live life to its fullest; aim for the stars yet celebrate wherever you actually land; in all ways, always assume the good intent of others as you seek the positive in all relationships; and be a good steward of your time in this body because time waits for no one, not even you my dear. Seek to thrive, not just survive.

I am so proud of you my love. My 6 foot 4-inch gentle giant paid attention. You are vibrant, joy-filled, peace-filled, socially conscientious, a lover of life, and fearless in your pursuit of your dreams wherever they may lead.

Dear Son, no matter what may happen in this world, continue to know your own bliss, your own path and your own truth. And never forget, God is always able. Love you my Little Camster!

Love Always...Mom

A Note to My Black Son Justin…

I have watched you grow into a responsible young man; you are smart, ambitious, caring strong and funny. I have watched how you are with your own son and I am very proud. The quality and quantity of time you spend with him is genuine.

Watching you me as a single mother, you always said "If I ever have a child, I will be there for him or her, no matter what!" just like I was and still am for you.

I wish all your dreams come true if you continue to keep God first and work very hard. You were never the kid that followed others; you were and still are the leader. You have always been your own man and I hope you keep it that way.

I will always support you and be there for you in any way I can even if we do not always see eye-to-eye, you will always be Mama's man (insider).

Love Always…Ma

A Note to My Black Son Steven, III, Pooter…

I find myself constantly in prayer for you my Son because the world that we live in seems to be afraid you the color of your skin.

I often wonder how to tell you to navigate through a world where your complexion, gender, educational intellect and natural born gifts and talents intimidates others who are of a different complexion than yours.

I then begin to remember what I have always prayed since I found out that I was carrying you: I pray that you will always remember to treat others with kindness, respect and patience and that people would do the same for you in return regardless of the color of your skin, gender or anything else that makes them uncomfortable with you as a person.

I pray that God would continue to lead, guide and protect you when the road of life gets rough and you do not know what to do. I want to encourage you to be the man that God has created YOU to be. I want you to chase after every goal and dream that your heart desires and have fun while doing so.

Lastly, I want you to always remember that I am your biggest cheerleader for everything that you want to do in this life of yours and I look forward to seeing you achieve it all. I love you so very much Steven, III and I am proud of the Man you are becoming.

Love Always…Mommy

A Note to My Black Son Troy…

Troy, you are my only Son, first child and a true blessing to my life. What a creative, smart, strong, handsome and respectful young, Black Man you have grown to be. I am proud to call you my Son for so many reasons. You have a heart of a lion that lets me know that you will be that protector not only for me, but your family and hopefully a young lady of your choice (approved by me of course, lol) that can see all the qualities a young, Black Man should be. Fear not my Son as God is the head of your life and will help direct your path as far as your dreams may go. Know that life will throw you curve balls from every direction, but your Ma is never too far away for guidance. You are no one's slave in a cotton field, you are no one's thug in the streets and no one's prisoner in an institution and let us keep it that way. I pray that you have a successful life ahead; remember you are the star of your own destiny and desires in life. I love you My Black Son…

Love Always…Ma

A Note to My Black Son Carter, My Cart…

Mommy loves you sooooooo much! I prayed for you, your life, and your future before you were born. Carter you and I have always been very close; that is why I call you my Velcro. It has been a joy to raise you, my only child. From rocking you to sleep every night, to watching you grow into an independent and very mature 6-year-old. You have the right mixture of innocence, and fierceness! You ask more questions than I can keep up with, but I am oh so proud of your inquisitiveness and your need to know. Your care and concern for others is what the world needs right now and forever! I always pray that God protects who you are, your innocence and your heart, from the parts of this life that would try to rob you of all things good. My Son, always remember to get up and try again, and again, and again! Never stay down too long, bounce back, shake the dust off, keep pressing forward, and smile! Look for the good in others and in situations; and do good for others and in situations. Make it your purpose to be a light in this world. Also make it your purpose to be a person who seeks council from the right people, is accountable for your actions, consistently learns, grows, and continues to be a better version of yourself each day! Make sure to take the time to enjoy life, laugh, play and have fun!!! I have no idea what the future holds, but I am so excited and believe that God has great things in store for you and He holds your future. Always remember that you are first a child of God who is loved.

Love Always…Mommy

A Note to My Black (Bonus) Son Jalen...

Although you are not mine biologically, I love you as if you were. I came into your life when you were in the 2ⁿᵈ grade and now you are a college student. When I first met you, your Dad brought you over to work on a George Washington Carver project and presentation that was due the very next day; who knew that that one encounter would lead to many more homework assignments and projects (lol). I have watched you grow and mature into the man you are now (and are still becoming every day).

You are a young, Black Man in America. That title comes with such a heaviness that I wish I could take away from you but I know that I cannot; it is my job, along with the rest of your "village" to help guide your through. With that being said, I have a few nuggets for you to take with you along this life journey:

- ❖ *Always remember to walk and stand tall in your purpose; never shrink to fit in with what others believe or perceive you should be; you are capable of greatness.*
- ❖ *Try to find the good in everyone and every situation and grow from it.*
- ❖ *Learn to appreciate the gifts of knowledge your elders share with you.*
- ❖ *Life will throw you many curve balls but nothing beats a swing but a hit.*
- ❖ *Love those in your life with not only words but deeds as well because they will not be here always and you do not want to live with the regrets of not showing it to them.*
- ❖ *Remember, "in all things we (YOU) are more than conquerors through Him who loved us" (Romans 8:37-NIV).*
- ❖ *Never burn a bridge that you may have to cross again.*

I know that we have had our fair share of ups and downs over the years; I am grateful that we have persevered through them and come out in a positive place; I pray that you understand that everything was done and came from a place of love in hopes that you would be a better person. I wish you every good thing in life and pray God's covering over your life today, tomorrow and always.

Love Always...Toya

A Final Note to All the Black Sons…

There are a few things that we want you to always remember as you, our Black Sons, continue to on this journey called life:

- *Always pray and keep God first in EVERYTHING you do.*
- *I will always love and support you no matter what you do.*
- *When given a choice, always choose kindness and to dance.*
- *"Whether you think you can or think you can't-you're right." (Henry Ford)*
- *Always look for the good in people.*
- *Your mind is a garden; your thoughts are the seeds. You can grow flowers for you can grow weeds.*
- *"Our greatest glory is not in never falling, but in getting up every time we do." (Confucius)*
- *"Knowledge speaks but wisdom listens." (Jimi Hendrix)*
- *Do not compare yourself to others. There is not comparison between the Sun and the Moon. They shine when it is their time to do so; so will you!*
- *God's got this and God's got you which means you got this too!*

Here are some scriptures that will help you along in your journey:

Psalm 1:1-3 (NIV): Blessed is the one who does not walk in step with the wicked or stand in the way that sinners take or sit in the company of mockers, but whose delight is in the law of the LORD, and who meditates on his law day and night. That person is like a tree planted by streams of water, which yields its fruit in season and whose leaf does not wither— whatever they do prospers.

Psalm 118:6-8 (NIV): The LORD is with me; I will not be afraid. What can mere mortals do to me? The LORD is with me; he is my helper. I look in triumph on my enemies. It is better to take refuge in the LORD than to trust in humans.

I Corinthians 16:13 (NIV): Watch, stand fast in the faith, be brave, be strong

We pray every word in this book helps to inspire, be a source of strength and comfort and be something you can look upon in the time of need. Continue to shine and be great!

Love Always…All the Black Moms

Black Mom & Adult Son Illustration By: Rodney Potts

Made in the USA
Columbia, SC
29 May 2021